Honor Among Nations

ELLIOTT ABRAMS became president of the Ethics and Public Policy Center in 1996. During the 1980s he held three Assistant Secretary posts at the U.S. Department of State. He is the author of *Undue Process* (1993), *Security and Sacrifice* (1995), and *Faith or Fear* (1997).

Honor Among Nations
Intangible Interests and Foreign Policy

Edited by
Elliott Abrams

Essays by Donald Kagan, William C. Wohlforth,
Daniel J. Mahoney, *and* Karl Walling
Responses by Peter W. Rodman, Charles H. Fairbanks, Jr.,
Francis Fukuyama, *and* Robert Kagan

ETHICS AND PUBLIC POLICY CENTER
WASHINGTON, D.C.

The moral issues that shape foreign and domestic policy are central to the work of the Ethics and Public Policy Center. The Center is a non-profit institution established in 1976 to clarify and reinforce the role of the Judeo-Christian moral tradition in the American public policy debate. Its activities include research, writing, publications, and conferences. Current programs are Catholic Studies, Evangelical Studies, Jewish Studies, the Project on the Judiciary, the Program on Medical Science and Society, studies in religion and foreign policy, and the Marriage Law Project.

Library of Congress Cataloging-in-Publication Data:
Honor among nations: intangible interests and foreign policy / edited
   by Elliott Abrams; essays by Donald Kagan . . . [et al.]; responses
   by Peter W. Rodman . . . [et al.].
      p.   cm.
   Includes bibliographical references and index.
   ISBN 0-89633-188-1 (pbk.)
   1. World politics.   2. Honor.   3. Ethics.   I. Abrams, Elliott,
   1948– .   II. Kagan, Donald.
   D32.H66   1998   98-18569
   327—dc21   CIP

Ethics and Public Policy Center
1015 Fifteenth Street NW ✦ Washington, D.C. 20005
(202) 682-1200 ✦ *fax* (202) 408-0632 ✦ *website* www.eppc.org.

Contents

Preface

Professor Donald Kagan of Yale University, in his panoramic book *On the Origins of War,* quoted Thucydides' observation that "often some aspect of honor is decisive . . . in bringing on wars." In the nineteenth century, Britain used its sea power to stamp out the slave trade, an indication that the then reigning British interpretation of national interest included a weighty moral ingredient. Surely Charles de Gaulle would have defined French "vital interests" in this century in such a manner; his "certain idea of France" included far more than the possession of territory and military strength. Of course, it can be argued—and is, often strenuously—that departure from concrete definitions of national interest leads inevitably to dangerously expansive policies. Yet are the terms "vital interests" and "national security interests" any more precise, any less potentially expansive?

In 1996-97, with the generous support of the Smith Richardson Foundation, the Ethics and Public Policy Center undertook a project called "Just War After the Cold War." Much of its fruit appears in a larger volume entitled *Close Calls: Intervention, Terrorism, Missile Defense, and "Just War" Today,* published by the Center in 1998. The last of the four conferences in the project, "Intangible Interests and U.S. Foreign Policy," is the source of the essays in this second book.

The subject here is how nations, including our own, define their vital interests. In particular, the essayists ask whether "intangible" interests such as national honor, morale, and reputation can be deemed "vital." Can they be considered an essential part of a policy that seeks to defend "traditional" security interests? **Donald Kagan** begins the discussion with "Honor, Interest, and the Nation-State," to which **Peter W. Rodman** responds. **William C. Wohlforth** looks into the foreign policy of Russia (1600-1995) and its definition of national interests; **Charles H. Fairbanks, Jr.,** responds. The foreign policy of De Gaulle's France is the subject of **Daniel J. Mahoney** and respondent **Francis Fukuyama.** Finally, **Karl Walling,** with **Robert Kagan** responding, deals with the way in which the early American statesmen—especially Alexander Hamilton—balanced interest and honor, and asks what if any insights for today we can gain from those early debates.

These essays span centuries of foreign-policy making, from ancient Greece to the contemporary United States, and illuminate the defining of national interest in a new democracy, a savage dictatorship, and an ancient monarchy. No nation-state can escape the kinds of questions posed here. While statesmen may ignore them in the short run, eventually, as these essays suggest, the bill for this short-sightedness falls due. Like an individual or, in a closer analogy, like an army, nations have resources and weaknesses that go far beyond the physical. To be sure, the strength of a nation is measured in part in oil reserves, weaponry, GDP growth rates, and sheer size. But whether in the Peloponnesian Wars or the Cold War, the Battle of Britain or today's Persian Gulf, nations measure each other's determination, reliability, and morale as much as—or even more than—they count the size of each other's fleets. Such "intangibles" are, as these essays suggest, central to any calculation of national power.

— ELLIOTT ABRAMS

1

Honor, Interest, and the Nation-State

Donald Kagan

For the last 2,500 years, at least, states have usually conducted their affairs and have often gone to war for reasons that would not pass the test of "vital national interests" posed by modern students of politics. On countless occasions states have acted to defend or foster a collection of beliefs and feelings that ran counter to their practical interests and have placed their security at risk, persisting in their course even when the costs were high and the danger was evident.

The common practice of calling such motives "irrational" reveals how narrow the professional understanding of what matters to people has become in our day. The notion that only economic benefits, power, and security are rational goals is a prejudice of our time, a product of the attempt to treat the world of human events as though it were the inanimate physical universe, susceptible to scientific analysis and free to ignore human feelings, motives, and will. Such an approach is no more adequate to explain current behavior than to explain the actions of human beings throughout history.

Donald Kagan is Bass Professor of History, Classics, and Western Civilization at Yale University, where he has taught a popular course on the origins of war for over twenty-five years. His book *On the Origins of War* was published in 1995.

1

An entirely different collection of concerns and motives has dominated the relations between peoples and states since antiquity. The category is honor. It contains such elements as the search for fame and glory, the desire to escape shame, disgrace, and embarrassment, and the wish to avenge a wrong or disgrace and thereby to erase an embarrassment and restore one's reputation.

Some concepts of what is honorable and what is dishonorable remain the same over the ages, but others change, sometimes superficially and sometimes deeply, from place to place and over time even in the same place. Although other people's ideas of honor, especially those of an earlier time, can seem silly or outmoded, the surface elements often conceal a more fundamental similarity or even identity with those that still have force today.

Honor and the Competition for Power

The role of honor in international relations can be divided into two parts: (1) its place in the competition for power and tangible advantage, and (2) its function in establishing other goals—such as fame and glory—that are different from these more practical goals and often can be achieved only at their expense. When we translate "honor" into such terms as "deference," "esteem," "just due," "regard," "respect," or "prestige," its practical importance in the competition for power becomes evident. When the honor of a state wanes, so, too, does its power. When a state's power grows, the respect it receives is likely to grow, as well. Even when a state's material "objective" power appears to remain the same, it really declines if in some manner the attitudes of others towards it change. This happens most often when a state is seen to lack the will or courage to use its material power. So concern for honor is an integral part of the competition for power, and any analysis of international relations and war that ignores honor and fixes solely on purely political and economic issues must be inadequate.

The first man to observe carefully the relationship of power and honor was the Athenian historian Thucydides. Like the modern "realists," Thucydides understood international relations as the competition for power, and war as the resort to arms in that competition. But he went beyond most modern scholars in explaining why people seek power.

Thucydides found that in the struggle for power people go to war out of "honor, fear, and interest."[1] His account of the causes of the Peloponnesian War begins with a Corinthian challenge to the state of Corcyra, part of a continuing contest over disputed colonies. The Corinthians were determined to build a sphere of influence in the Greek northwest to compensate for their diminished prestige elsewhere. Corcyra's challenge to Corinthian hegemony there threatened to have practical consequences in the struggle for power: the loss of prestige in the area of competition and the consequent danger of defections by allies and other states in the region.

World War I and Honor

Threats to prestige that challenge the security of a state and give rise to the fear, anger, and hatred that lead to war are common throughout history. Honor in this sense played a critical role in the coming of the First World War. After the First Balkan War of 1912, a newly powerful Serbia emerged as a threat to the existence of the Austro-Hungarian Empire. During the peace conference the Austrians' policy was that Serbia must be contained: the Austrians needed to "reassert the monarchy's 'prestige.'"[2] When Serbia held to its territorial demands, even the Hungarian prime minister, usually opposed to military intervention, conceded that the issue was "whether Austria-Hungary was a 'viable power' or had fallen into a 'laughable decadence.'"[3] An Austrian ultimatum forced Serbia to back down. But victory in the Second Balkan War in 1913 brought Serbia new confidence. Humiliated by the Austrian ultimatum, the Serbs were eager for revenge.

The Austrians increasingly saw the Serbs as a menace to the existence of the empire. After the Balkan Wars, the Austrians had no choice but to pursue a policy of prestige; they were too weak to do otherwise. Failure to change the perception of weakness could well lead to the disintegration of the empire. And so, as has often happened throughout history, a policy of prestige turned into a policy of interest.

In the final crisis of 1914, Russia was moved by similar considerations. The Russian foreign minister, Sergey Sazonov, argued that if the Serbs accepted Austria's ultimatum it would mean the abandonment of Russia's "'historic mission [to gain the independence of the Slavic peoples], she would be considered a decadent state and would henceforth have to take second place among the powers,' losing

'all her authority' and allowing 'Russian prestige in the Balkans' to
'collapse utterly.'"[4] Russia's material interests in Serbia and the other
Balkan states were not great, but the Balkans were the place where its
power and reputation were most on display and at risk. The state of
its prestige made it either more or less able to defend its clients and
press its claims about such fundamental matters as access to the Straits
(the waters connecting the Black Sea to the Aegean, hence the
Mediterranean), and more or less attractive as an alliance partner to
those states on whom it depended for security. Defense of its prestige
was thus the defense of a most important interest, and fear of the loss
of prestige the most powerful motive for risking war.

In a similar way, Great Britain's concern for its honor and for the
danger that dishonor posed to its safety played a large role in the
decisons taken by the British government prior to the war. In his
famous Mansion House speech during the second Moroccan crisis of
1911, David Lloyd George said:

> I believe it is essential in the highest interests, not merely of this
> country, but of the world, that Britain should at all hazards main-
> tain her prestige among the Great Powers of the world. . . . I would
> make great sacrifices to preserve peace. I conceive that nothing
> would justify a disturbance of international good-will except ques-
> tions of the greatest national moment. But if a situation were to be
> forced upon us in which peace could only be preserved by the sur-
> render of the great and beneficent position Britain has won by cen-
> turies of heroism and achievement, by allowing Britain to be
> treated, where her interests were vitally affected, as if she were of
> no account in the Cabinet of nations, then I say emphatically that
> peace at that price would be a humiliation intolerable for a great
> country like ours to endure.[5]

Both during the crisis of 1914 and in his reflections in later years,
Britain's foreign secretary, Sir Edward Grey, made it clear that he was
moved by the same considerations. In August 1914 he told Parliament
that Britain could keep out of the war by issuing a proclamation of
unconditional neutrality, but that he rejected that course:

> If we did take that line by saying: "We will have nothing whatever
> to do with this matter" under no conditions—the Belgian Treaty
> obligations, the possible position in the Mediterranean, with dam-
> age to British interests, and what may happen to France from our

failure to support France—if we were to say that all those things mattered nothing, were as nothing, and to say we would stand aside, we should, I believe, sacrifice our respect and good name and reputation before the world, and should not escape the most serious and grave economic consequences.[6]

Years later he wrote, "The real reason for going into the war was that, if we did not stand by France and stand up for Belgium against this aggression, we should be isolated, discredited, and hated; and there would be nothing for us but a miserable and ignoble future."[7] To be sure, Grey and the British were moved by fear of the dangers Germany presented to their most vital interests; but they could be made to face up to those dangers only when they understood the danger to their honor.

Honor, then, in the sense of prestige, clearly plays an important role in the competition for power. But nations also react strongly to the fear of dishonor, to assaults on their dignity that are the result of passion and hatred, not calculation. Thucydides' account of Corinth's quarrel with Corcyra, a colony the Corinthians had founded, emphasizes such a motive. The Corinthians became involved in an unimportant civil war on the fringes of the Greek world "out of hatred for the Corcyraeans," for the Corcyraeans "paid no attention to the Corinthians even though they were their colonists. In the common festivals they did not give them the customary privileges, nor did they begin by having a Corinthian commence the initial sacrifices, as the other colonies did, but treated them contemptuously."[8] Thucydides speaks of a passion, not calculation. No economic interest, no competition for power, no threat to security, no practical fear can explain the Corinthians' behavior. It was the affront to their honor and dignity that caused them to act.

Such feelings are of course not confined to the distant past. In 1935 Mussolini was determined to avenge the humiliation suffered by the Italian army at Adowa in Abyssinia some four decades earlier, one of the rare defeats suffered by a European power at the hands of a non-European nation. It remained "a shameful scar," in the words of the poet Gabriele D'Annunzio; the memory "hammered in [the] head" of Mussolini for years.[9] Neither economics nor demographic needs, but only the search for vengeance and the restoration of lost honor, lay behind the war on Abyssinia.

Honor and the Avoidance of Shame

Mussolini's Abyssinian campaign reminds us of the second important aspect of the place of honor in international relations, for he undertook it also "as a means of glorifying the Fascist regime"[10] and restoring to Italy the glory of the ancient Roman Empire. In the form of "fame," "glory," or "grandeur," honor motivated decisions about international relations and war and peace for millennia. These concepts represent the goals and values that, it is thought, not only are good in themselves but must be pursued and protected in order to avoid shame. In the heroic world depicted in the *Iliad,* Achilles prefers to fight at Troy, where he knows he must die, than to stay safely at home and be immortal, because to stay at home would deprive him of the undying fame and glory that alone make life worth living for a hero. In dynastic ages, kings risk the prosperity and security of their kingdoms and themselves to extend or preserve their territory or to avenge insults, all to achieve glory and avoid humiliation. In religious eras, crusading kings do the same in the name of the true religion. What is less obvious is that peoples and leaders of our own time are moved by the same motives. It is just that some different concepts are at the root of their sense of what honor requires.

In speeches during the war, Pericles told the Athenians that they were fighting for the honor and glory that bring a kind of immortality. The dead warriors "won for themselves the praise that never grows old and the most distinguished of all graves, not those in which they lie, but where their glory remains in eternal memory."[11] Honor in this sense was a powerfully effective motive for the citizens of the Athenian imperial democracy. To make the sacrifices needed to conduct an effective foreign policy, the common people in the assembly must believe in the value of the cause and the actions it requires.

In sixteenth-century Europe, during the struggles of the Reformation and Counter Reformation, religion was often the most important repository of honor, the test of a leader's character and quality. Philip II, ruler of the Spanish Hapsburg Empire, provides the best example. Applying a twentieth-century outlook to the events of earlier times, some modern scholars have attributed the ruin of this great empire to excessive military expenditure caused by "strategical overstretch," presumably in search of power and practical advantages.[12] But an understanding better founded on contemporary evidence explains the fatal policy as "a messianic imperialism . . . driving the king to elevate religious principle above common sense."[13]

The growth of Protestantism in the Netherlands led Philip to begin and sustain the long, terrible war there, a running sore that drained Spain's strength for the rest of his life. Ministers and advisers repeatedly warned him about the deadly material consequences to his and Spain's interests. Philip answered that "the cause of religion must take precedence over everything."[14] On Philip's foreign policy rested his salvation, his glory, his honor. He would see his empire bankrupt and ruined before giving up these intangible interests.

By the next century, the core of the European monarchs' sense of honor was the advance or retreat of the reputations of their dynasties. In the words of one Spanish minister, "A monarchy that has lost its reputation, even if it has lost no territory, is a sky without light, a sun without rays, a body without a soul."[15] In 1914, as we have seen, Lord Grey said much the same thing, if less poetically, about a democratic Great Britain. At the turn of the eighteenth century, rulers like Charles XII of Sweden, William III of England, and Louis XIV of France "were all determined not to leave the state entrusted to them diminished and more defenseless than when they received it: this would be the ultimate blot on their own *gloire*."[16]

Cynical dismissals of such motives are naïve. The evidence shows that royal pursuit of glory was essential to what the politically significant part of the population expected of a king. Failure to pursue glory would be a breach of honor, a disgrace that would undermine the king's legitimacy and his right to conduct the affairs of the state. As one scholar points out, "Prestige and glory were the basis of the power of early-modern monarchs both domestically and in international relations."[17]

Louis XIV and Honor

Nothing better illustrates the power of honor—in the sense of glory and reputation—as a practical interest in those times than the career of France's Louis XIV. This shrewd French monarch knew the practical value of glory in the competition for power on the international scene. "Reputation," he said, "is often more effective that the most powerful armies. All conquerors have gained more by reputation than by the sword."[18] Yet the pursuit of glory was not merely a useful tool in the competition for power or more tangible benefits. Louis's three great wars against coalitions of European powers were disastrous from the perspective of what is now called national interest. They ruined the kingdom's finances and put strains on the society that ultimately brought down the monarchy itself.[19]

The most costly and disastrous of these wars was the War of the Spanish Succession. Louis clearly understood the costs and dangers of undertaking a war against a coalition that included the Habsburg emperor, England, and the Netherlands, and he spent years negotiating agreements for the partition of the Spanish empire so as to avoid war when the sickly and childless king should die. But when the Spaniards offered their throne to Louis's grandson, concern for his own and his dynasty's glory and honor would not let him refuse. "He ventured French fortune and lives . . . knowing full well that the crowns of France and Spain would probably never unite. It was enough for a Bourbon to rule Spain."[20]

It would be easy to conclude that the pursuit of such impractical goals—of honor instead of interest—is what brings disaster in foreign policy, and that adherence to more prudent goals limited to "interests" would avoid such disasters. But whatever we may think of that judgment, people throughout history have thought otherwise. They have often given great weight to honor as an interest, both as an element in the competition for power and as something valuable in itself. Ordinary Athenians and other Greeks of the Classical period willingly risked their lives for the fame that would bring them collective immortality. Romans of the republic fought wars to gain or uphold the *dignitas* that brought honor to their ancestors and glory to themselves. Kings of early modern Europe fought to advance the honor and glory of their dynasties and the glory of God.

The French Revolution unleashed the new and violent force of nationalism, which gave a powerful impetus to an old concept of honor in international relations. That concept tied honor to solidarity with one's ethnic brethren, their union in a single nation, and the pursuit of that nation's dignity and reputation in the competition with others. The pursuit of national goals since the French Revolution at the expense of peace, prosperity, and security is a tale too well known to need repeating here. Campaigns for the establishment, expansion, and defense of national states undermined the system established at the Congress of Vienna in 1815. The statesmen who shaped that system, we are told, sought to preserve the peace by the rational balancing of power, but their deeper purpose was to preserve the honor and values they cherished against the danger posed by the new forces of nationalism and democracy. Only for this were they prepared to forgo the old competition for dynastic power. Before very long, however, their system failed. Ideology, in the form of nationalism in place of religion or dynastic ambition, had become the focal point of honor in the modern world.

Kaiser William II and Glory

The career of Germany's William II shows how the search for glory combined with the new nationalism to produce a new meaning for honor in international affairs—and with explosive power. Bismarck had devised a European international system that kept the peace and guaranteed German security, but after his discharge, forces in Germany pressed for something greater, if less tangible: the pursuit of world power and prestige. In 1914, after two decades of competition in armaments and increased international tension leading to crises and even to wars, Germany's Chancellor Theodor von Bethmann Hollweg repeated a complaint that had been often used by his kaiser and other dissatisfied Germans: "[Germany] is forced to expand somehow or other; it has not yet found that 'place in the sun' which is its due."[21]

Advocates of these ideas demanded expansion, colonies, and a navy, the symbol and instrument of *weltpolitik* and greatness. As one perceptive scholar has put it, what the Germans really wanted was "*Geltung* [respect], *Anerkennung* [recognition], *Gleichberechtigung* [equal authority], a whole host of emotionally loaded and psychologically revealing objectives."[22] It is hard to escape the sense that Germany's demand for colonies and world empire was based far less on a concern for "interest," in Thucydides' language, than on the search for "honor."

William fired Bismarck and embarked on the road to glory. The center of his new course was to build a great navy capable of matching the British. As one biographer has put it,

> the German fleet was to him not so much a calculated ingredient of domestic or foreign policy but a romantic emblem of Hohenzollern glory. . . . A navy was to him a gorgeous apparition through

which to humble Germany's enemies and create respect and riches both for ruler and people. . . . Without a navy the kaiser knew that he could take no effective action in either the Atlantic or the Pacific and that this impotence would lead ineluctably to a humiliating decline in Germany's prestige as well as his own. He therefore must have a fleet.[23]

Germany's great naval program soon provoked a naval race of unprecedented size and cost, a diplomatic revolution that saw the emergence of two antagonistic power blocs and played a vital part in bringing on the war and the destruction of German power. It also created financial and political problems that forced the kaiser to think repeatedly of a *coup d'état* to save the regime. William pursued this policy that brought destruction to his regime internally and externally in a manner not very different from that of Louis XIV, except that it was powerfully supported by the new intelligentsia and bourgeoisie in the name of the German nation.

The New 20th-Century Sense

The twentieth century introduced a new sense of honor into international relations. The new era was marked by a struggle between increasingly democratic states and tyrannies or dictatorships. The victors in the Great War were democracies, and the expanded requirements of total war made it essential to gain and sustain the support of the whole people. They and many of their leaders were increasingly committed to a new set of ideas as to what is moral and honorable in international affairs. War itself was widely believed to be morally wrong, and its causes were believed to be connected with the expansionism and aggressiveness natural to authoritarian and despotic regimes.

People in the democracies thought that democracy was right and good not only in itself but also as a force for peace. Over time they came to believe that only a war in defense of democracy and self-determination was just. Many became convinced that democracies had a responsibility to stand together against aggression and despotism. Woodrow Wilson was not inventing anything when he made the defense and extension of democracy and the rejection of autocracy a crucial aim of the war. The victors rejected the authoritarian regimes of their opponents, insisting that "military autocrats" and the "king of Prussia" could not take part in peace negotiations.[24] In the public mind of the winning nations, autocratic, militaristic, undemocratic states were illegitimate. They could be expected to undertake aggression, which must be resisted.

A new device appeared for resisting aggression and keeping the peace: collective security in the form of the League of Nations. This was not merely a new version of older coalitions like the Quadruple Alliance of the nineteenth century. It was the product not of private negotiations among a few diplomats but of great, open, public discussions, supported by politicians, public associations, and widespread propaganda. It meant to include all the nations of the world, and it involved a commitment to resist aggression whenever it appeared. Political leaders might regard all this cynically, but they and their successors in the democracies would need to deal with a public opinion that took it seriously. In the Western countries, especially in Britain, the need to uphold collective security, to resist aggression, particularly by non-democratic regimes, was attached to the concept of national honor. Any political leader who ignored this new public belief would do so at his peril.

Honor vs. Appeasement

Italy's attack on Abyssinia in 1935 reveals the critical role of honor in this new sense. Before the Great War, a European assault on a weak African nation of no interest to any of the other European powers would not have provoked any serious reaction from any of them. The creation of the League of Nations, however, and the accompanying commitments to collective security and to resistance to aggression changed the situation. Although the British government had little sentiment for a strong stand against Italy, there was a considerable feeling that the League could not be abandoned. The average Briton had accepted the actions of his government since the end of the war on the understanding that it was not retreating from honor and responsibility but seeking a course based on higher principle. A policy that seemed cynical and cowardly could not long be sustained; yet there was great reluctance to antagonize the Italians.

Britain's foreign minister Samuel Hoare and France's Pierre Laval had agreed that no real effort should be made to stop Mussolini, but such a decision could not be admitted to the British public. Hoare, therefore, felt compelled to assert that "the League stands, and my country stands with it, for the collective maintenance of the Covenant in its entirety, and particularly for steady and collective resistance to all acts of unprovoked aggression."[25] This was empty bombast for public consumption at home. Hoare quickly communicated to Mussolini that Britain was eager for a settlement, had no wish to humiliate Italy, and would neither employ military sanctions nor close the Suez Canal.[26] Reassured, Mussolini rejected further proposals for compromise and invaded Abyssinia on October 3, 1935.

Italian success in Abyssinia brought political and public pressure that pushed the Cabinet to the point of approving an oil embargo, so Hoare produced the Hoare-Laval agreement, meant to provide a peaceful settlement without risking such a provocation. The deal was widely seen as a reward for aggression, a blow to the idea of the League and collective security, and an act of cowardice. Hoare was forced to resign. Lloyd George personified the disgust felt by the British people toward their own government's behavior when he pointed to the members of the Government on the front bench and said: "Tonight we have had the cowardly surrender, and there are the cowards."[27]

Some British leaders were prepared to sacrifice Abyssinia, as Britain would almost surely have done in previous centuries. But this, as Correlli Barnett, points out, "was 1935, not 1835 or 1735. English foreign policy was no longer a matter simply for the foreign secretary or even the Cabinet."[28] By 1935 the British public would not ignore the commitment to resist aggression, especially on the part of a dictator against a weak country. A government trying to ignore that conviction would be rejected as not only mistaken but also, as the reaction of many Conservatives and of Lloyd George made clear, dishonorable.

The efforts of Neville Chamberlain two years later to conduct his policy of appeasement, ostensibly based on hard-headed calculations of interest and a rejection of ideology, ran into the same new reality, intensified by the intervening dishonor and its consequences. Chamberlain portrayed his intended abandonment of Czechoslovakia as a matter of practicality and common sense, but he soon ran into trouble. One cabinet member was indiscreet enough to raise the question of honor: the required concessions were "unfair to the Czechs and dishonourable to ourselves." The opposition Labour and Liberal parties made their case, "not on strategic grounds, but on the score of morality and ideology. A robber power—and, what was worse, a Fascist power—had been positively helped by the British Government to enlarge itself at the expense of a small country, and, what was worse, a democratic country."[29]

Rumblings from his own party and the country at large forced Chamberlain to change his public tone. His declaration that "any attempt to dominate the world by force was one which the democracies must resist" was greeted with enthusiasm. It soon became clear that the British people would no longer put up with appeasement and weakness but demanded a new policy of resistance and strength. The tenor of the criticism revealed that the new resolve came from a sense of shame and anger over honor betrayed more than from a need to protect British interests.

In this atmosphere, fearing the charge of inaction, Chamberlain gave way to over-reaction. To escape the charges of shame and dishonor, his government took actions that were both vain and foolish, offering guarantees to Poland and other states that it could not enforce. Finally Hitler's attack on Poland forced Britain to enter a war for which it was still ill prepared, one for which it had no realistic strategic plan, and one, we should not forget, that it came within a hair's breadth of losing. Chamberlain and his colleagues, it is well known, misjudged the true nature of Hitler and the threat he posed, but they also badly misunderstood the new realities of international relations conducted by democratic nations. The public would not tolerate the dishonor that came from allowing aggressive dictatorships to overrun autonomous, democratic nations.

The fall of Norway and Denmark in the spring of 1940 finally forced Chamberlain from office in disgrace. The new leader, Winston Churchill, had long focused on the dishonor of the appeasement policy, and he firmly rejected a relatively generous peace offer from the apparently victorious and irresistible Hitler. Churchill's policy accurately reflected the feelings of most of the British people, who preferred the risks and suffering of a terrible war to the dishonor of a shameful peace with a cruel dictator who personified ideas and institutions that were anathema to them.

The Cold War and the Rise of Realism

Britain's example has broader relevance. In spite of attempts to discredit it during and since the war in Vietnam, the "Munich analogy," relying heavily on the sense of dishonor inherent in appeasing expansionist dictators, has been a major force in shaping the policy of the United States, the heir to Britain's leadership after the Second World War.

The confrontation with the Soviet Union after the war was certainly a contest for power and involved important elements of fear and interest, but a conflict of values and ideas invoking questions of honor was no less important. To most Americans and their leaders, the Soviet Union was an aggressive, militaristic dictatorship not very different from the ones just defeated, a dangerous enemy of freedom and democracy; its occupation of central and eastern Europe was no less offensive. Not only American security but also decency and honor argued for its containment, if not its defeat. The American people would not have accepted compulsory military service, higher taxes to pay for increased armaments, a permanent European alliance, and the Korean War without motives that went beyond material interest.

Passionate anti-Communism, the determination to resist Communist expansion anywhere in the world, even the intention of defeating the Soviet Union and international Communism resulted from the conviction that honor, not merely interest, was at stake. The rise of such feelings appalled and alarmed the cognoscenti, who feared that the untutored emotions of the democratic masses would lead to dangerous crusades, the exhaustion of America's resources, or war and mutual annihilation. The "realist" school emerged and insisted that foreign policy should rigorously eschew such feelings arising from what I have called questions of honor. It should deal only with calculable questions of power and interest; it should be kept in the hands of educated experts who would seek to measure these things accurately and to restrain their uninformed and immoderate fellow citizens. The "realists" accepted the permanence of the Soviet Union and world Communism, seeking to find areas of accommodation. When the balance of power seemed to be shifting in favor of the Soviets they adopted a policy they called détente, which seemed to others more like retreat and appeasement.

This produced not accommodation from the Soviets but more aggressive expansion and great gains in the arms race that upset the balance of power still further. Some Americans regarded détente not merely as mistaken but as a dishonorable retreat. The Soviet invasion of Afghanistan and the Iranians' seizure of American hostages swung most Americans behind that view and helped sweep its opponents from power. The new regime was committed to the restoration of American strength and honor. Rejecting the received "realist" wisdom, the new president called the Soviet Union an "evil empire," predicted its defeat and collapse, and set in motion an increase in armaments meant to help bring victory and honor. To the surprise of the cognoscenti, this was followed by neither economic implosion nor suicidal war but by the collapse of the Soviet Union, the discrediting of Communism and dictatorship, and the vindication of freedom and democracy. Ordinary Americans considered this outcome an honor to their values and institutions that justified the effort and sacrifice it had required.

That happy outcome could never have been achieved merely by the pursuit of what the experts considered to be practical national interests. The uniquely persistent and costly policy of engagement in the world could not have been maintained without the widespread commitment of the people at large to values that were deeper and more humanly compelling than concern over economic and geopolitical advantage. In acting from these motives, they were behaving not with the stubborn ignorance of the untaught but as people have normally done throughout history.

"Realists" are right to point to the centrality of the contest for power in international relations, to the dangers of imprudence and immoderation arising from the pursuit of such intangible goals as honor. But experience shows that the competition for power itself, however rationally calculated and pursued, is no less dangerous. It, too, calls for moderation and restraint, and it provides no better guarantee of a happy result. The fact is, however, that power is never pursued for itself but always for some deeply held value more understandable to ordinary human beings—often honor in the senses we have used it. The mistake of the "realists" is not their interest in the struggle for power but their deliberate neglect of everything else, especially the non-scientific, contingent, very human feelings and beliefs that most powerfully move people.

In modern states where there is direct or representative democracy it is not possible to exclude issues of morality and ideology from consideration. That is how the ordinary citizen thinks about affairs, both foreign and domestic; the politicians cannot afford to ignore their feelings. And in fact the politicians, with few exceptions, think the same way. Arguments about morality and ideology involve what Thucydides called honor, something that nations from antiquity to the present have not been able to ignore. To exclude such considerations is the height of fantasy and the opposite of realism.

A Response

Peter W. Rodman

I am here to defend the "honor" of the realists, if that is a possible formulation and a possible mission.

I have the greatest respect for Professor Kagan's paper and all of his other work. His analysis of history and his illumination of the "intangible" factor are brilliant. Toward the end, however, his critique of realism seems to some degree to be an attack on a straw man. I think there is greater compatibility between the notion of power and the notion of honor than he gives credit for. Each one, properly conceived, has to take account of the other.

Someone I know who wrote about the Congress of Vienna spent quite a lot of time on the concept of *legitimacy*—an intangible factor, defined as a shared sense of the justice of the international order.[1] I don't know of any realist who would discuss the nineteenth century without taking into account this intangible factor that held it together. As we know, of course, the equilibrium was not stable in the end. But what sustained it for a long period of time was a shared sense not only of the justice of the international arrangements but of the rightness of the internal arrangements.

Peter W. Rodman is director of national security programs at the Nixon Center for Peace and Freedom, Washington, D.C., and a senior editor of *National Review*. He held national-security posts under four presidents.

One of the most disruptive challenges to a concert of powers is ideology. That also is a part of the realist analysis. Napoleonic France, or even Soviet Russia in the later period, serves as an example of the realist understanding of the salience of values: it's not a dismissal of ideology but a recognition of its power. The most sophisticated realist, I would emphasize, has long understood the truths that Dr. Kagan is pointing out.

In addition, sometimes it is very hard to separate the factor of calculation from the factor of honor as he describes it. For example, sometimes a foreign-policy challenge that occurs in some remote location is properly understood as the harbinger of a more fundamental challenge. When South Korea was invaded in 1950, we had no defense commitment to that country. But leaders of the West saw that this invasion had enormous implications that went far beyond the Korean peninsula. It signified a new boldness on the part of Stalin. It certainly had implications for the West—especially if the West did not react in some fundamental way.

I see Kuwait in 1990 as very similar. We had no defense treaty with Kuwait. But as soon as the attack happened, we saw correctly that this was a hostile power making a bid for hegemony in a vital region. Whatever our assessment beforehand, after the fact we understood exactly what was at stake, even though this calculation involved both matters of interest and matters intangible. Especially in the nuclear age, shifts in the global geopolitical balance are more likely to come about from an accumulation of small advantages than from some single apocalyptic assault. This is another intangible. We're talking here about an assessment of a trend, an assessment of the direction of history. It is subjective to some degree, but to some degree it is not. It's how one sees the shifts in the balance of power—or events on the margin that reveal something about the intentions of an aggressor. This is how statesmen measure things. It's not the physical GNP figures—it's an assessment of a dynamic, of intangibles of *will*.

Kagan mentioned the factor of will as part of his analysis, and it is quite clearly a part of mine. Power, sensibly understood, equals physical strength multiplied by the political will to use it. This is an insight of enormous importance, and one that is hardly unknown to strategists of the traditional school. It is one explanation, for example, of how the American superpower—big and powerful as we are—has appeared weak in certain situations, not because our GNP was down but because our political will to use our power was in doubt. The same factor of political will explains why a small country that is objectively weak, like France or Syria, can turn itself into a major player in the international arena by a kind of sheer force of will—by stubbornness in the case of the French, or ruthlessness in the case of the Syrians.

The mirror image of will is called *credibility*—that is, others' perception that you are willing to use your power. Your enemies believe your warnings, your friends believe your reassurances—if you have credibility. Your warnings and reassurances don't have to be tested every other week. Having credibility is a way of shaping reality.

During the Vietnam War, I served in an administration in which the president (Nixon) and the secretary of state (Kissinger) harped on this theme that American credibility was on the line. A great power upon which other countries rely for their security cannot long remain in the great-power business if it gets into the habit of abandoning allies under pressure. This notion was much derided at the time by the wise men of the academy. Credibility was thought to be a function of the vanity or pigheadedness of our leaders. Arthur Schlesinger and others used to say that the United States would be better off if we just abandoned Vietnam; we would be applauded in the world, we would be admired.

The administration did not take this view. "Peace with honor" was the phrase. An honorable settlement, an honorable outcome—this was the vocabulary in which the administration defended its commitment. If you did a NEXIS search of the use of the word "honor" in recent episodes of American foreign policy, you probably would be overloaded with references from the Nixon administration. (I know because I wrote a number of them.) Nixon and Kissinger—those hard-headed advocates of U.S. national interests—were adamant in their conviction that our reputation for reliability was a fundamental element of our strategic position.

Fifteen years later, after Saddam Hussein invaded Kuwait and before the Gulf War, the Iraqi press and a lot of Iraqi diplomatic communications were filled with references to Vietnam and also Lebanon—two instances where in Saddam's view the United States had shown that its word didn't count for all that much, that it lacked staying power. In fact, before the invasion of Kuwait, Saddam said something in these terms to our ambassador, April Glaspie.

Fortunately, he turned out to be a bit wrong. But credibility, once you lose it, has to be re-earned the hard way.

I think the realist and the idealist are, at a basic level, on the same side here. An appreciation of honor and an appreciation of power are both integral to a realistic understanding of the world. The intangible has to be a part of the calculation. Reductionism in either direction is wrong.

Even more, I would say that we are together against the naïve. We are standing together against the escapists who evade considerations both of interest *and* of honor. We are together against the intellectually superficial who imagine that the world is governed by abstract virtue, and against those on the Left who believe that American self-denial is the basic prerequisite of peace. American strength, American credibility, American will, American honor, America's faith in itself—all these go together. Together they are the foundation of our leadership in the world and our strategic position.

2

Honor as Interest in Russian Decisions for War, 1600-1995

William C. Wohlforth

Rightly to be great / Is not to stir without great argument,
But greatly to find quarrel in a straw / When honor's at the stake.
—*Hamlet*, IV, 4, 53

In the life of states just as in that of private individuals there are
moments when one must forget all but the defense of his honor.
—Tsar Alexander II, February 1877

Should states fight for straws when honor is at stake? Few are the
wars fought for national survival or obvious profit. In many if not
most wars, statesmen cannot articulate tangible stakes that are commensurate with the blood and treasure sacrificed for victory. Appeals
to intangibles like honor, reputation, and prestige are therefore common in history. Many such appeals are obvious rationalizations for
miscalculations—wars begun for a modest strategic gain become wars
for the national honor when the enemy is discovered to be better prepared than expected. But, as Donald Kagan shows in his book *On the*

William C. Wohlforth is an Olin post-doctoral fellow in international
security studies at Yale University. He is the author of *Elusive Balance: Power
and Perceptions During the Cold War* (1993). He formerly taught politics at
Princeton.

Origins of War, leaders frequently expect beforehand that the tangible costs of war will exceed the tangible gain and yet choose war nonetheless.[1]

Russia is a clear case in support of Kagan's generalization. On many occasions in the history of the Russian Empire, the tsar and his ministers chose to fight even when, in the privacy of their war council, they could not identify tangible interests at issue commensurate with the expected costs and risks of war. The meeting of the Council of Ministers at Tsarskoe Selo on July 24, 1914, at which Nicholas II agreed to accept the risk of war against Austria–Hungary and Germany in support of Serbia, is a dramatic example. Despite their clear understanding of Russia's weakness after its defeat by Japan in 1904–5 and the revolution of 1905, despite their expectation that Russia's relative power would increase in the years ahead, despite their lack of tangible or strategic interests in the Balkans, Nicholas and his ministers took their empire to war.[2] Russia's prestige, they reasoned, could not stand further concessions to the Central Powers. The decision brought Russia into a conflict that led to the destruction of everything those men who met on July 24 held dear.

But the meeting of July 1914 was neither the first nor the last such gathering in Russian and Soviet history. Russians have paid dearly for their leaders' commitment to honor. From Peter the Great's decision in 1701 to avenge his defeat at Narva the previous year, through the decisions of Nicholas I and Alexander II that Russian prestige demanded showdowns with Turkey in 1827, 1853, and 1877, to Khrushchev's risky gambits in Berlin and Cuba and Brezhnev's expensive involvements in the Third World in the 1970s, Russia's rulers have taken risks, spilled their subjects' blood, and emptied Kremlin coffers for the honor, prestige, or reputation of the state.

The question I address in this essay is, Was the game worth the candle? Was honor an interest or a delusion? *Given* (and it is important to stress this assumption) the Russian leaders' goal of building and then maintaining a huge empire, was the concern with honor as Kagan defines it ("deference, esteem, just due, regard, respect, or prestige") truly in the vital interest of the state? Or was it a "myth of empire," to use Jack Snyder's term, that led only to self-destructive behavior on the world scene?[3]

I argue below that the case for honor-as-myth has not been made, though most scholars of Russian and Soviet foreign relations think it has. And while I cannot claim to make the case for honor-as-interest in the confines of this essay, I do intend to forward a preliminary brief on its behalf, if only to go on record against the overwhelming bulk of scholarly opinion. In other words, I seek to show how a reasonable person might suspect not only that the Russian leaders often meant what they said when they claimed to fight for honor, but that they were often right to do so. Far from being a myth of empire, the willingness periodically to fight for honor may have been a necessary condition of empire.

At first brush, my first task might appear hopeless. After all, a growing body of empirical literature in international relations makes a strong case that exaggerated concerns for reputation are not warranted by evidence or logic. For these scholars, "honor and reputation," as well as associated strategic beliefs such as the "domino theory," the belief in "offense dominance" over defense in war, and the belief in "bandwagoning" (strength attracts allies), are now and should remain discredited intellectual anachronisms. These scholars have shown how these ideas led to disasters on the international scene, from World War I to Vietnam.[4] They have undercut the assumptions underlying these ideas through careful research.[5] They have forwarded theories that explain why decision-makers claim to believe these discredited notions, focusing on domestic interest groups or cognitive or social-psychological biases.[6]

Moreover, these arguments resonate with specialists in Russia's foreign relations. Russia has a reputation for poor grand strategy. The Russian Empire and its Soviet successor paid very large costs on the world scene, fighting numerous wars and engaging in a great many expensive rivalries with other states. Despite these sacrifices, St. Petersburg and Moscow suffered serious reversals of fortune, with both empires eventually collapsing in part because of the great burdens imposed on them by international competition. And Russian rulers have often cited honor or other intangible interests as a *casus belli*. This combination of high costs, ultimate failure, and frequent references to the importance of intangible interests has led many political scientists and historians to see Russia as an example of the practical application of strategic myths. Russia would have done much better, the argument goes, had its leaders paid less attention to intangible interests. Obsession with honor and prestige simply embroiled the empire in conflicts with more advanced powers and drained the government's reserves of wealth and legitimacy, paving the way for state breakdown and revolution.

Despite the strength of this literature, I argue that it has failed to confront two issues. First, it has not given due consideration to the reasons statesmen actually put forth for treating intangibles as vital interests. As a result, scholars frequently import into the analysis their own belief that security ought to be the only goal of states. Having smuggled in this normative assumption, they can easily show that much strategic behavior and the ideas underlying it are self-defeating. And, second, the general scholarly literature that deals with the problem of intangible interests—whether it supports or opposes the proposition that honor can be a rational state interest—systematically underestimates the empirical challenges it faces. I treat these issues in the next two sections, and then turn to a revisionist account of Russia's strategic history that follows from this analysis.

WHY 'FIND QUARREL IN A STRAW'?

> We lost thirty thousand dead in Korea to save face for the United States and the United Nations, not to save South Korea for the South Koreans, and it was undoubtedly worth it. Soviet expectations about the behavior of the United States are one of the most valuable assets we possess in world affairs.—Thomas Schelling[7]

> The prestige of power means in practice the glory of power over other communities . . . [and] it is on this prestige that the consensus of specific action of legitimacy is founded.—Max Weber[8]

When explaining a state's decisions to incur costs of war that seem disproportionate to the immediate issue at hand, statesmen frequently refer to a coherent set of arguments that recurs through history. The most fundamental claim they make is that the intangible factors—honor, prestige, and reputation (what Schelling called "face")—are an important element of a state's strategic interest, if not the most important element. This claim contradicts the notion that honor, fear, and interest can be disentangled. Indeed, in traditional diplomatic parlance, the terms "prestige," "honor," and "vital interests" have often been used as synonyms.[9] Statesmen generally do not argue that it is necessary to fight for intangibles for their own sake but rather that fighting for intangible interests now will bring tangible benefits, or prevent tangible costs, over the long run. If the state's reputation is respected in the councils of great powers, the argument runs, it will benefit more in international politics and pay fewer costs overall. Avoiding war now could well be a false economy if by so doing the state squanders its reputation and thereby encourages future challenges under worse circumstances.

These arguments are rooted in an observation so obvious to statesmen that they rarely feel the need to articulate it: namely, that international politics is a social realm in which peoples' beliefs are basic determinants of reality. Our position in this society of states is determined in part by what others think of us. Our actions are meaningful mainly as they affect the beliefs and expectations of other members of the society. These beliefs are structural constraints; they help determine our security, status, and prosperity in international affairs. They may require us to refrain from actions that would bring tangible gain, and they may demand that we take very costly actions that appear to bring scant tangible gain. Indeed, tangible factors, such as strategic territory, colonial possessions, and armaments, may actually be subordinate to intangibles like reputation or prestige.

These notions are familiar to all students of deterrence theory. A state's security is partially a function of the credibility of its deterrent, and that credibility is composed of a material force posture *and* the government's reputation for resolve. Preventing attacks on the state itself or on its allies may require expensive fights on small issues in order to maintain the reputation for resolve. However, anyone familiar with the international politics of periods other than the Cold War and of countries other than the United States encounters a serious problem with the deterrence literature: it captures only a small proportion of states' strategic behavior, and consequently is only one (often not very important) rationale statesmen use to explain the apparently disproportionate costs of wars. Decision-makers must be concerned about preventing physical attacks on their state or its allies, but over long periods of international history such threats are diffuse and conjectural. Meanwhile, there is no shortage of other issues to worry about in international affairs.

Deterrence and Deference

In addition to deterrence, governments also care about *deference,* that is, the degree to which their interests are accommodated by other states. Where deterrence concerns security, deference concerns status. In the social system of states, as in any other social system, a status hierarchy emerges: dependent powers, middle powers, and great powers, with more or less contested rankings within each group. High status confers tangible benefits in the form of decision-making autonomy and deference on the part of others concerning issues of importance to one's security and prosperity. The higher a given state's status, the more other states adjust their policies to accommodate its interests.

The deterrence of threats and war is a serious business, but it often is a background consideration rather than an immediate concern. Status, on the other hand, is felt keenly every day by government officials at all levels who deal with the outside world, from the sovereign to his or her ministers and ambassadors. Indeed, even the humblest citizen, who never ventures abroad, may derive spiritual and material gain from the international prestige of his or her state. Since the success or failure of all international policies, however grandiose or mundane, is crucially dependent on status, any self-interested government must see constantly to the preservation or improvement of its position. If these policies are adopted for the security and welfare of the populace, or some politically important portion of that populace, then they, too, arguably have a stake in the state's position in the international hierarchy.

Because the hierarchy of states emerges within a general systemic anarchy where no authority can stop states from resorting to force, theorists such as Ralph Hawtrey, E. H. Carr, A. K. F. Organski, and Robert Gilpin have regarded military power as the fundamental source of status. In their formulation, rank in the hierarchy of states is determined by prestige, which, according to Carr, is simply "the recognition by others of your strength."[10] As in some animal realms, where walruses or wolves battle for preeminence, in this understanding of the international realm states must fight to prove their strength in order to attain and maintain status. If fighting a war can bring increased prestige (or prevent loss of prestige), then the costs of that war have to be measured not against the immediate issue at stake but against all the diplomatic benefits that accrue over time by virtue of the state's having stood firm (or against all the diplomatic losses that would have accrued over time had the government refused battle).

The proposition that status is conferred *solely* on the basis of military prowess is debatable. Surely, economic, technical, and cultural factors also help determine status independent of their implications for military power. The requisites of status have varied across different international systems in history, and they change over time within systems.[11] In the modern states system, the relative importance of military factors in determining status may be declining.[12] Nevertheless, for long reaches of international history—prominently including the formative years of the Russian Empire—military strength was the *conditio sine qua non* of inclusion in the great-power club.[13] The rules for entry were simple and brutal: to belong, you had to defeat a current member in war.[14]

The Internal Analogues

All arguments about deterrence and deference have *internal* analogues that may apply to many states but are especially relevant for multinational empires. Governments maintain their rule through some combination of legitimacy and a reputation for coercive sanction. The weaker the state's bases of legitimacy, and thus the weaker the habitual deference to its rule on the part of its subjects, the more salient the state's reputation for coercive sanction. Thus, the same reputational logic that may rationalize the costly use of force externally has often been deployed to explain disproportionate state violence in domestic contexts. As potential international systems waiting to be born, empires face a particularly acute form of this problem. The imperial sovereign needs to maintain his or her reputation and prestige among groups within the empire that may defect. As contiguous land empires in an age of nationalism, when the legitimacy of imperial rule waned, Austria-Hungary, Ottoman Turkey, Romanov Russia, and the Soviet Union faced especially acute problems of internal deterrence and deference. And, as the histories of these empires make plain, the requisites of internal deterrence and deference intersected and constrained external policies in important ways.

Russian rulers (and their counterparts in Constantinople, Vienna, and Moscow) appealed to classic reputational arguments concerning the need to maintain an image of invincible power domestically to

justify many costly policies, including the brutal use of disproportionate force to teach "lessons" to those groups constituting a real or
perceived threat to the empire's integrity. An infamous but typical
example is General Mikhail Skobelev's rationalization for his brutal
massacre of Turkmen tribespeople (women and children were promi-
nent among the casualties) in 1882:

> I hold it as a principle, that in Asia the duration of the peace is in
> direct proportion to the slaughter you inflict on the enemy. The
> harder you hit them, the longer they will be quiet afterwards. We
> killed nearly 20,000 Turkomans at Goeke-Tepe. The survivors will
> not soon forget the lesson.[15]

Similar words have been uttered by similarly placed officials in many
other empires through history. As reprehensible as these policies of
internal deterrence are, their supporting logic and frequently bloody
consequences are identical with their external counterparts.

The logical symmetry between external and internal deterrence is
particularly strong in empires, where internal deterrence is aimed at
groups who are connected to a specific territory but lack a state.
And often empires also have to pay a high price externally for the
internal image of invincibility. True, with the important exceptions of
Ottoman repression against Christians and Soviet repression in East
Central Europe, direct domestic deterrence of the Skobelev variety
did not usually incur high costs internationally. But domestic reputational concerns were a powerful constraint on foreign policy more
generally, with high external costs clearly recognized by imperial elites.

In Russia's case, the Polish problem is an example. For almost two
centuries, Russian fear of a Polish uprising was a constant constraint
on St. Petersburg. In 1812, Napoleon bragged that his Grand Duchy
of Warsaw, recognized by Alexander in the Tilsit treaties of 1807, was
a pistol aimed at Russia's heart, and Alexander agreed, concluding
that he had to break out of Tilsit at nearly any cost. Thereafter, Russians ruled out many concessions and many military strategies that
they may have thought optimal for external purposes for fear of their
consequences for the touchy Polish question.[16] Needless to say, precisely these concerns reemerged in East Central Europe after the
Second World War. Concern that external concessions on the German Question or other issues in European security could destabilize

the Warsaw Pact was a staple of Cold War Soviet policy, as were the high costs Moscow had to pay internationally for its internal reputation for resolve.

Thus the arguments for treating honor as a vital interest go beyond the realm of Schelling (quoted earlier on U.S. "face-saving" in Korea) and deterrence to encompass status, deference, and the international and domestic benefits they provide. As Max Weber argued early in the century, since external and internal reputations are linked, success and failure abroad feed back into domestic stability. If these arguments are to be believed, then the ruler who cannot or will not pay the costs necessary to maintain the state's reputation may soon face challenges from within and without.[17]

Honor is one among many motivations for war, and the fact that governments frequently cite it is not a reliable indicator of its true importance. As many scholars note, reputational arguments may serve as covers either for miscalculations or for corrupt policies whose true motivations cannot be revealed. However, there is no obvious reason to believe that statesmen exaggerate honor as a motive for war in public. It is quite possible that they underreport the frequency with which they are moved by concern for intangible interests. References to tangible interests may be covers for decisions truly motivated by intangibles. In each case, what decision-makers say both at the time and in retrospect depends on some mix of what they really believe and what they think will sell. And, as I show in the next section, appeals to intangible interests are quite hard to substantiate, a fact that may have led many statesmen to conclude that they would be hard policies to sell to their publics or to historians.

EVALUATING THE CASE FOR HONOR AS INTEREST

The most frequently asked question about international politics is: Why do states behave in such costly ways? Why do they engage in expensive wars, arms races, and rivalries? Statesmen answer with a coherent set of arguments that focus on intangible interests. The problem with these arguments is common in international politics: they are superficially plausible, and cannot be refuted merely by an appeal to logic, but it is extraordinarily hard to evaluate their truth either in general or in particular cases. And the stakes are the highest imaginable, measured in the hundreds of thousands of human lives sacrificed in the name of intangible interests. Intellectuals are surely right to be skeptical of these arguments. However, justifying this skepticism by appeal to the evidence runs into three sets of problems.

■ First, the general argument that honor often must be treated as an interest is much broader and covers a much greater range of strategic behavior than is encompassed by the American literature on deterrence theory. A scholarly treatise that demonstrates in a particular case or in several cases that a government's concern for honor or reputation did not contribute to its security does not necessarily defuse the argument. Even if an analyst can show that a government systematically harmed its narrow security interests over a prolonged period by engaging in too much costly behavior in world politics—a hard case to make—this does not necessarily undercut the government's rationale for its policies. It may have been fighting for prestige among states, even at the sacrifice of immediate security.

Contemporary scholarship notwithstanding, security is but one goal that states pursue. If a government faces a trade-off between security and prestige, it may not always resolve the trade-off in favor of security. A relatively invulnerable great power may be willing to accept some security costs in order to achieve major status gains. The classic example is a state whose leader, believing its relative power is increasing, seek to translate these capabilities into heightened status. In so doing, the government risks eliciting counterbalancing behavior from other states. If a prestige-enhancing policy produces counterbalancing—in short, a pattern of decisions that seems self-defeating from a pure security perspective—but also yields increased deference, the trade-off may have benefit the government overall.

■ Second, these arguments are matters of human judgment, not science. Decisions concerning intangible interests are always made under conditions of high uncertainty. The decision-makers involved are calculating the effect of their actions on other human beings with whom they interact on the international stage and over whom they rule. The scholar who renders a severe judgment on the sagacity of such decisions with the sure knowledge of how everything turned out must always ask: What, if not hindsight, provides me with a special insight concerning these complex matters of judgment, an insight superior to that possessed by people on the scene? This is not to imply that statesmen are never wrong. On the contrary, it is to say that they are wrong quite frequently. Decision-makers operating under high uncertainty will inevitably miscalculate. While uncovering such miscalculations is important and useful, it does not constitute a case against the ideas that informed those decisions.

To demonstrate that a belief in the need to defend honor or reputation is a misleading "myth," one must do more than connect the belief to some faulty decisions. Since decisions are made under conditions of uncertainty, any belief can be connected to miscalculations. Governments do not say that honor always requires sacrifice, just that it does from time to time. To evaluate this belief in general, one need only show that honor matters often enough in important enough ways that a sensible government will have to take the idea seriously. Once the initial plausibility of the idea is accepted, it follows that the strategic history of all great powers will contain examples where the costs of defending reputation exceeded the benefits. The existence of such cases is alone insufficient to discredit the belief. Instead, in order to demonstrate the "mythical" status of a state's commitment to honor, one must show that the relative costs of the commitment over time exceeded the relative costs of a similar commitment to another belief that would also have served the government's ends.

■ Third, measuring the relative costs of a commitment to defend honor is much harder than scholars often realize because reputational arguments create daunting problems of selection bias. The *only* part of the argument that is easy to observe and measure is the concrete costs paid in the form of wars fought, weapons purchased, and so on.[18] The rest of the story—if it is true—takes place off stage: benefits are reckoned in bad things that never happen, such as wars never fought and challenges never made owing to a firm reputation, and in good things that are very hard to measure empirically, such as increased status and the diplomatic advantages it conveys.

Most studies of war study wars. That approach virtually guarantees the conclusion that war is senseless. Theories of war make powerful statements about times of peace. Reputational arguments say that any given war is both the *culmination* of a long series of decisions based on assessments of intangibles like resolve, and the *beginning* of a new series of decisions based on new assessments of intangibles that are influenced by the war's outcome. It is impossible to evaluate these arguments by exclusive or even predominant focus on wars. Indeed, these arguments cannot be evaluated by exclusive focus on observable behavior and outcomes.

HONOR AND REPUTATION: RUSSIA AS
A SUCCESS STORY

Empirical studies of intangible interests that endeavor to face these challenges seriously are hard to come by. As noted earlier, the American literature is centered on deterrence theory, which tends to exclude all concerns of status from its analysis. Questions of *internal* deterrence or deference are almost never addressed. Studies that do not take deterrence theory as their point of departure tend to rely instead on neo-realist theory, which focuses exclusively on security as a goal of states.[19] Quantitative works, while they cover many cases, generally have difficulty addressing issues of intangible interests, which defy easily reproducible measurement. Historical case studies, which are best suited to capture intangibles, tend to focus on one or a few cases, usually wars or crises. This concentration on only those instances where costs are paid guarantees the conclusion that states tend to exaggerate the importance of intangible interests.[20]

These methodological concerns prompt questions and point to evidence concerning Russia's strategic history that are rarely addressed by those who see it as a case of self-defeating myth-mongering. In this light, let us consider the various arguments used to justify the high costs exacted by concern for intangible interests.

Argument 1: Status and Prestige

External deference is the place to start, since for most of its 400-year existence the Russian Empire was expansionist. As Russian defense minister Prince A. N. Kuropatkin noted in a strategic *tour d'horizon* written for the tsar in 1900, most of Russia's wars had been wars of aggression, and most had been prosecuted successfully.[21] Between the fifteenth century and the end of the nineteenth, the Russian Empire expanded at an average rate of 130 square kilometers a day—or one present-day Holland per year.[22] Some of these wars were justified by reference to prosperity or security: the riches of Siberia beckoned; strategic ports or rail junctions often lay nearby in foreign territory;

secure borders often seemed one offensive away from the current frontier. But those motives miss a large part of the story: Russia's struggle for status. In both its Romanov and Soviet forms, the Russian Empire had to fight its way into the great-power club as an outsider from the wrong side of the tracks. Because of their initial status outside of European society, St. Petersburg and Moscow may have faced particularly arduous terms of entry.

In discussions of Russia's strategic history, the struggle for status as one rationale for many of the scores of wars that accompanied the rise of the Russian empire is often missed. Surveying Peter's reign, for example, the liberal Russian historian Michael Florinsky observed:

> The incredibly costly wars of Peter are often represented as the more or less inevitable and in the end beneficial stages of the inexorable historical process which eventually led to the creation of a unified empire with outlets on the Baltic and on the Black Seas. . . . A closer examination of the facts . . . leads to the highly unsatisfactory conclusion that the wars which filled the reign of Peter were largely of his own making, that they were embarked upon without any realization of what they actually meant, and without any definite and clear object in view.[23]

Florinsky misses a third explanation of Peter's wars, one rooted in a widely held interpretation of the tsar-Westernizer: his well-documented desire for Russia to "take its just position in Europe."[24] In this explanation, the "clear object" in Peter's view was less this or that strategic outpost or seaport than the fundamental goal of membership in the European society of states. Whether Peter achieved this objective in his lifetime can be debated, but few diplomatic historians would disagree with the observation that pre-Petrine Russia was not a member of that society and that the Russia of Peter's widow Catherine I—or at least that of their daughter Elizabeth—most certainly was.[25]

Russian prestige grew in the late eighteenth century with the numerous wars of conquest launched by Catherine II. After Alexander I defeated Napoleon's Grand Army in 1812, the Russian Empire was perceived as the preeminent land power in Europe and, with the British Empire, one of the two most significant states in the world. As most conventional histories have it, Russia's defeat of revolutionary France secured St. Petersburg's reputation for several generations. The *leitmotif* of nineteenth-century diplomacy was fear of Russian power, and yet, with the exception of the Crimean War, St. Petersburg managed to enjoy the prestige associated with this perception of its power without provoking a balancing countercoalition. In hindsight, these perceptions of Russian power seem exaggerated. As impressive as 1812 was, it was soon contradicted by evidence from Nicholas's campaigns in Turkey and his disastrous performance in Crimea. Nevertheless, thanks in part to a vigorous policy of spin-managing and prestige-assertion, the reputation stuck. Thus one interpretation of Russia's grand strategy in the nineteenth century, at what might be considered the apex of its career as a great power, is a stunningly successful policy of living beyond one's means by brilliantly nurturing a reputation for power.

Of course, Nicholas I will not get pride of place in anyone's book of great statesmen. In 1853, his bluster and intimidation landed him in a war against a coalition of Turkey, Britain, France, and Piedmont, supported diplomatically by Sweden and the Hapsburg Empire. "Honor," as his foreign minister Count Nesselrode wrote, "does not oblige us to hurl ourselves into a bottomless abyss."[26] But Nesselrode expressed that view after the war had begun, when the costs of the policy he had helped engineer had become clear. Nicholas's perceived need to assert his prestige against Turkey and France by means short of war followed directly from the policy that had been in place since 1814, perceived in Russia and elsewhere as a formidable success. As Nesselrode himself had written in 1850, "since 1814 the position of Russia and of its sovereign has not been either more favorable [*belle*] or more noble [*grande*]."[27] Asserting prestige in the 1853 crisis was surely a costly mistake (equally so on the part of London and Paris). But if it followed two hundred years of building up Russian prestige through military victory and four successful decades of defending and preserving the influence won in 1812, it looks much more like a rational miscalculation than the reflection of a deeply entrenched bias or attachment to an obviously misleading strategic myth.

The Costs of Crimea

A study of Russia's prestige policy would need to examine the years after Crimea very closely. The tangible stakes of the war were hard to name. The consequences of the war for the Eastern Question were negligible. And the costs were horrific: a half million Turkish, Russian, British, and French lives. But in the opinion of many Russian statesmen at the time and historians later, the less easily measured stakes of the war were immense, measured in the diplomatic price Russia had to pay every day over the next twenty years. With only a bit of his habitual hyperbole, A. J. P. Taylor sums up a widely held reckoning of these costs: "After 1856 Russia carried less weight in European affairs than at any time since the end of the Great Northern War in 1721; and the predominance which she had exercised at Berlin and Vienna before 1854 she was never to wield again until 1945." Indeed, Taylor notes, Britain and France would not have proposed such draconian terms of peace "to any Power whom they regarded as truly European."[28] Thus the intangible stakes of Crimea may have been nothing short of all the status achievements of Peter and Catherine.

If Taylor's assessment is even half-right, it is little wonder that subsequent Russian statesmen sought to recapture at least some of the international status they had once possessed. Now, however, concerns of status and prestige became ever more entwined with external and internal security. If the Napoleonic Wars had transformed Russia into a conservative power, the Crimean War made it into a defensive one. Russians feared that further loss of status internationally not only would be costly in itself but would lead to security costs as the other great powers and internal national groups both increased their demands on St. Petersburg.

These considerations explain why Alexander II, who was dismissive of pan-Slavism and generally uninterested in further imperial expansion, nonetheless accepted another war against Turkey in 1877. When they met in February of that year, neither Alexander nor his ministers could identify tangible state interests at stake in the Balkans. Nonetheless, the tsar summed up the discussion: "In the life of states just as in that of private individuals there are moments when one must forget all but the defense of his honor."[29] According to William Fuller, the tsar's reference to "honor" reflected the analysis of General Staff strategist N. N. Obruchev, who had argued that a tough line on Turkey was necessary for Russia's prestige:

In Obruchev's opinion, Turkey had to be compelled to make concessions to the Christian provinces of its Empire. If Russia demobilized its forces without achieving them, this would "almost correspond to a second lost Crimean campaign" in terms of the decay of Russia's international standing that might result. As Obruchev saw it, the costs of the war (high as they were) were still lower than the costs of refusing to fight.[30]

Obruchev and his sovereign might have been wrong. As things turned out, Russia won a less than decisive victory, and achieved at the 1878 Congress of Berlin less than it had hoped for (and thought it had secured in the treaty of San Stefano). But assessing Obruchev's argument is not as simple as comparing the terms of the Berlin treaty with what the most optimistic Russians had hoped to achieve. His argument called for a different calculation: a comparison between Russia's fortunes on the international scene after 1878 to what those fortunes would have been like had Russia backed down in the face of the Turks' repressions in their Christian provinces. In fact, Russia's diplomatic position not only did not deteriorate further, as Obruchev had feared it would if St. Petersburg did not face down the sultan, but actually improved substantially after 1878. Taylor asserts confidently that "Russia recovered in 1878 what she had lost in 1856."[31] Indeed, Russia's standing had recovered to such an extent by the turn of the century that it was once again being touted as the coming superpower of the new age. So strong was this impression that even the defeat at the hands of the Japanese and the subsequent revolution of 1905 succeeded in suppressing it only for a few years.[32]

The Soviet Pursuit of Prestige

Soviet Russia did not fight the "wars for prestige" that its tsarist predecessor had. But Moscow did pay heavy costs internationally and exact horrific costs domestically for international prestige. Weakened and ideologically suspect, the Soviet Union was excluded from the normal society of states just as was "Asiatic" pre-Petrine Russia. But the Bolsheviks set for themselves a much tougher task than the Romanovs ever faced. Not only did they want to be treated as a great power, with commensurate influence over security arrangements, but they also sought to change the rules of the international game to permit their "dual policy" of state-to-state relations above and revolutionary activism below.

Incredibly, Stalin and his entourage had largely succeeded by the late 1930s, as all the powers had recognized Moscow and the two competing capitalist camps were vying for Stalin's favors. Military victory in World War II brought such prestige that the Soviet rulers felt justified in comparing their world position with Tsar Alexander's after the defeat of Napoleonic France.[33] Stalin and his successors then sought over the next forty years to translate military power into security *and* increased deference without fighting, while at the same time maintaining some commitment to revolution. And once again, despite a comparatively small economy and many other disadvantages, they managed to attain from the other great powers very high levels of deference without ever unambiguously sacrificing their ideology.

As critics point out, Moscow paid dearly for this policy. Arms buildups, crisis brinkmanship, and expensive adventures in the Third World not only overextended Kremlin finances but also helped forge a worldwide anti-Soviet coalition of states that by the early 1980s included all the other great powers. However, any assessment of Soviet foreign policy needs to consider its stunning achievement in building status. The Soviet Union's status increased in each decade from the 1920s until the 1970s. Until the 1980s, the Western powers were continuously on the defensive, despite their massively superior economic, military, and technological potential. The much maligned Leonid Brezhnev, for example, took power at a time when Western economies were booming and the United States was engaged in a furious military buildup. In a scant seven years, he and Gromyko had attained a favorable *modus vivendi* with West Germany and had secured international recognition of the German Democratic Republic, the post-war sphere of domination in East Central Europe, and most of their wartime conquests. What is more, they were engaged in a détente with the world's preeminent power, the United States, on formal terms of parity.

If the goal had merely been security, the Soviets might well be accused of having subscribed to self-defeating strategic myths. They might well have been better off hunkering down in Eurasia and not seeking to compete with the United States, just as Peter the Great might have done better had he been content to remain tsar of a backwater Asiatic state lying well off the beaten track of world politics. But the goal was not merely security. Soviet leaders also wanted to influence world politics and to retain some fealty to the ideas on which their state was founded. They found that building up military power delivered these goods. Scholars may someday show that the policies Soviet leaders followed ill served their objectives, but they have yet to do so convincingly.

Argument 2: External Deterrence

As an expanding empire, Russia viewed security as a secondary concern over long stretches of its history. Nevertheless, after the empire had composed itself, it suffered five invasions: by the French in 1812, the French, British, and Turks in 1853, the Germans in 1915-17, the Allies in 1918-19, and the Germans again in 1941. Because most of the action in deterrence takes place in peacetime, in preventing wars and challenges, looking just at these invasions is virtually guaranteed to bias the result against the proposition that fighting for reputation pays. Wars are deterrence failures, and studying them will lead to the conclusion that deterrence fails. Yet even a restricted look at just these invasions actually supports the argument that Russia's concern for reputation was rational.

In 1812, Napoleon decided to invade a Russia that he had beaten on the battlefield and whose tsar had chosen to bandwagon with him at Tilsit in 1807 rather than suffer further defeat. By seeming to be amenable to compromise, Alexander fed Napoleon's belief that inflicting enough punishment on Russia would lead to an offer for negotiations. Thus, on the classical deterrence variables of capabilities and resolve, Russia seemed ripe for the picking. Realizing his mistake, Alexander had to fight a decisive war to reestablish Russia's reputation for military power and his own reputation for resolve. As we have seen, this decision brought spectacular results.

The situation came close to repeating itself in 1941. Stalin ruined the Soviet Union's reputation for power by purging the military, and then chose to bandwagon with Hitler in 1939. Although Hitler may have been undeterrable, the evidence he had as of 1941 was that the Soviet Union was dramatically weaker than it seemed on paper and that its leader was likely to cave in to superior force.

The other three cases are mixed. Crimea is the sole clear deterrence failure; Nicholas's efforts to project an image of implacable resolve and formidable fighting power failed to compel the Turks to comply and then failed to deter the highly resolved and capable Western powers from invading. The German and Allied invasions in World War I were clearly driven by assessments of capabilities rather than resolve.

Evaluating the deterrence argument in the manner most biased against it, we find substantial support for it. Of the three major, life-threatening invasions of Russia, two followed policies of appeasement that may have signaled lack of resolve. And in both of those cases, the leaders who eventually decided to fight uncompromisingly to the end were richly rewarded by a significant and lasting increase in their state's status in world affairs.

Argument 3: Internal Deference and Deterrence

Arguably the most critical question and perhaps the most difficult to evaluate is the extent to which Russia's very survival as an empire depended on its reputation for ruthless resolve. Is the fact that the Russian empire collapsed in 1917 and 1991 an indication of policy failure or success against the odds? Russia's breakdown is often read as an "ultimate" failure; that reading influences the interpretation of policies that appear to have lead to that outcome. The policies of the late Romanovs and the post-war Soviets can be made to look absurd in light of the evidence concerning Russia's real power revealed by its performance in World War I and the collapse of Communism in 1989-91. But this same evidence can be used to demonstrate how extraordinarily hard the task was of holding the empire together in the first place. Viewed in this light, Russia's extraordinary career of imperialism would look like a dramatic success story against all odds. The policies associated with that success would then appear presump-tively sound, and the burden of proof would be on those who sought to question the sagacity of Russia's prudent concern for its honor and reputation.

Of course, weaving knowledge of an outcome into the interpreta-tion of history is an unsound practice, whether one reads the out-come as evidence of success or failure. But posing the question about success or failure underscores the fact that hindsight is a double-edged sword. It reminds us that how we pose the problem—whether we choose to consider Russia's blundering decline and fall or its odds-defying longevity—goes a long way in determining the answers we find. In addition, it is fair to ask of a body of scholarship that it try to reconcile itself with other, formidable bodies of theoretical and empirical scholarship. Those who argue that Russia's obsession with prestige and honor was damaging to its interests are contradicted by a mass of scholarship describing Russia as a bizarre and precarious anachronism: an empire in the age of nationalism, a backward, inefficient, feudal Asiatic despotism competing on a level playing field against highly efficient, modern, industrial nation-states.

Shelves groan under the weight of tomes that testify to the inevitability of Russia's decline and fall, and strongly imply that St. Petersburg's and Moscow's obsession with reputation was founded in the realities rather than the myths of empire. Modernization theory, theories of nationalism, sociological theories of revolution, various economic theories of empire, even the formal theory of "principles and agents" all add up to one conclusion: Russian and Soviet rulers faced an impossible task in trying to maintain an empire.[34] Fighting a losing battle, sooner or later they were going to get surrounded and beaten by the forces of modernization and nationalism. Meanwhile, many of these same literatures strongly demonstrate the importance of a reputation for resolve in creating the domestic deterrence and deference that were necessary conditions of imperial survival.

On domestic deterrence, social theorists from Lenin to Skocpol have posited a causal link between failure in war and social revolution.[35] Defeat in war catalyzes and accelerates underlying processes of decline and decay of imperial states by breaking down the habitual deference to authority of subordinate classes and national elites. These groups must always calculate the costs and risks of defection from the state, and the regime's performance in war provides powerful evidence of its capability to sanction deviant behavior. Furthermore, while it would be going too far to say that power determines legitimacy in this literature, it is clear that the two are seen as closely connected. Defeat undermines the regime's legitimacy, undercutting its claim on the allegiance of its subjects and the effectiveness of the institutions of rule.

If this literature is true, an imperial government's reputation for power and resolve is one of the sinews that hold the empire together. It was probably less dialectics than experience that led Lenin to this conclusion, since Russia's defeat in war was often followed by domestic instability—a connection most dramatically demonstrated after the disastrous war with Japan in 1904.[36] The upshot is that imperial rulers should not embark on war lightly, but, if they do find themselves at war, they must not be perceived to lose. This consideration helps to explain persistence in wars after it is discovered that the calculation of the balance of power prior to the war was inaccurate. Thus in 1854, 1877, 1905, and, most dramatically, 1914, though the pre-war assessment of power was quickly proved wrong, Russian rulers nonetheless kept fighting. Part of the reason was surely the concern for external prestige, but internal deterrence and deference figured as well.

On internal deference, the matter of principles and agents is key.[37] Needing resources from the peripheral dominions, the imperial center appoints governors to see to it that a portion of the local economic surplus is returned to the empire. The governors face incentives to divert resources to local interests. The center confronts a continual problem of how to secure deference and loyalty from its agents deployed throughout the empire. Part of this deference is a function of the center's reputation for fierce resolve to defend its priorities, and that reputation occasionally must be secured by willingness to fight externally and internally. In addition, maintaining internal deference places limits on the concessions that can be made externally. If the imperial authorities are seen within the empire as being on the defensive externally, all the problems of securing deference are compounded, and the empire gets progressively weaker.

Bearing this literature in mind, what is a declining empire supposed to do? Each option presents different risks. None is a fail-safe answer to the problem of decline. (1) A declining empire should seek powerful external allies. But playing the alliance game may involve the empire in a war that could spell defeat and revolution. That was the lesson of 1914. (2) A declining empire may also try to expand in order to increase its security, enlarge its access to material resources and markets, and enhance its internal and external prestige. But that poses the same risks of war and revolution as acquiring allies, as was demonstrated in 1904-5. (3) The empire may try withdrawal and retrenchment internationally and decentralizing reform domestically. But that course damages international and internal prestige and usually ends up exacerbating the principle-agent problem. The maps of Latin America, Central Europe, the Balkans, and now Eurasia are littered with states whose independence was partially the result of the decentralizing reforms of long gone empires. In short, the decline of multinational empires is something approaching an empirical law of world politics, and all policy items on the menu of decline are unpalatable.

The decline and fall of the Soviet Union may serve as an illustration of these arguments. The perception of Moscow's willingness to enforce its dominion in Central Europe militarily appears to have been a necessary condition of its external empire. In 1953, 1956, and 1968, Soviet rulers decided to pay the international costs of repressing perceived or anticipated defection. But during the 1970s and 1980s, Moscow also responded to the classic problems of the decay of its imperial rule by devolving considerable authority to local agents in Central Europe and in the Union Republics of the USSR. By the time Gorbachev took the helm, the policy of dealing with principle-agent problems by increased decentralization was already well entrenched.

Gorbachev's response combined continued devolution in Central Europe with intermittent efforts at recentralization in the inner empire. Externally, he began to implement a policy of careful appeasement that required dispelling external perceptions of the Soviet threat. This proved to be a volatile mix of policies: dispelling the Soviet threat abroad did deliver détente, but it also dispelled Moscow's reputation for resolve in the outer empire, which rapidly became unglued. The collapse of the outer empire then fed into the center-periphery struggle in the Soviet Union itself, as Moscow's centralizing effort to control local agents clashed against its declining reputation for coercive sanction.

Gorbachev tried the policies of retrenchment and reform that are clearly the preferred option of the many scholars who argue that statesmen systematically exaggerate the importance of reputation. On balance, those policies should be applauded for minimizing the bloodshed that accompanied the end of the Cold War and the collapse of the Soviet Union. But it does need to be pointed out that those policies failed miserably in achieving Gorbachev's goals. It is simply much more difficult than is often realized to make the case that Russia was too concerned with protecting its prestige and too reluctant to consider retrenchment and reform as solutions to relative decline. When Nicholas II decided in 1914 to fight for prestige, his empire collapsed. When Gorbachev declined to fight for prestige and banked instead on retrenchment and reform, his empire collapsed. The two decisions and their consequences speak volumes about the intrinsic difficulty of the task both men faced. The argument that Russia was too concerned with its prestige suggests that alternative policies were available that could have maintained the empire longer, or as long at smaller cost. The voluminous literature on imperial decline suggests otherwise.

Concluding Observations

The argument that it is well and good to die for the honor of one's country should always be treated with healthy skepticism—especially when the person making it is not volunteering his or her own life, children, or property for the cause. In any given case, it is quite possible that the argument is wrong: it may well be put forth as a cover for some other interest that is difficult to articulate and defend publicly. And even if the argument is true for some definition of the state's interest, that definition may be highly suspect. Fighting for honor from time to time may be a necessary condition of great-power status—but perhaps a state can and should choose not to be a great power. Or, fighting for honor may be necessary to attain and maintain a high status in the hierarchy of world politics—but perhaps such status simply is not worth the sacrifice. Or, as in the case of Russia and the Soviet Union, the willingness to spill blood for the reputation of the state may be a necessary condition of empire—but maintaining an empire may not be a desirable or worthwhile goal.

Unfortunately, we probably know much less about the status of intangible interests than we think. They may be more or less important motives for war than the available evidence suggests. We may yet uncover a systematic propensity to exaggerate their importance. However, that case has yet to be made. We do not have a body of scholarship that tells us with certainty that appeals to honor, prestige, or reputation are necessarily disingenuous or wrong. For all we know, people who say these things may mean them, and if they act on these convictions they may be rewarded rather than punished.

As dangerous as these arguments can be, they need to be taken seriously and studied carefully. The assumption that reputational arguments are necessarily wrong or always disingenuous itself contains certain dangers. We may find ourselves incapable of understanding the behavior of others who claim to be motivated by intangibles. Russians are once again speaking the language of honor as interest. They are decrying their nation's humiliation and its ill treatment at the hands of the other great powers. This may be rhetoric for domestic consumption. It may be a cloak for the malign interests of lingering imperialist elites. Or it may reflect a genuine strategic assessment. If the latter is the case, then the consequences of policies such as the eastward expansion of NATO may turn out to be more lasting and costly than we realize.

A Response

Charles H. Fairbanks, Jr.

To begin with, I emphatically agree with William Wohlforth that the concerns in Moscow are now fundamentally about status and that realists' theory is a very poor prism through which to view those concerns. But let me talk about the paper in a more orderly way.

The theoretical part was extremely intelligent. Wohlforth stated the basic principle very well—that "international politics is a social realm in which peoples' beliefs are basic determinants of reality." It's also true, one can add, that people are reluctant to abandon their beliefs even in a direction that nominally they would prefer. Nobody took great advantage of the weakness of Russia after the Russo-Japanese War and the revolutionary upheavals of 1905, just as nobody took great advantage of the weakness of the United States after the Vietnam War. That shows how powerful and how lasting these beliefs or images are. It's also quite true that high status confers decision-making autonomy and the deference of others, which are important in foreign policy.

I was also persuaded by Wohlforth's methodological arguments, especially the argument that the benefits of going to war must be

Charles H. Fairbanks, Jr., is Research Professor of International Relations at the Paul H. Nitze School of Advanced International Studies, Johns Hopkins University, Washington, D.C. He is also director of the school's Central Asia Institute.

45

reckoned in part in terms of bad things that never happen, such as potential wars that are never fought. That is the fundamental weakness of most isolationists' arguments in the current American debate. Oddly enough, it undermines many of the internationalists' arguments, too, in that they take as a given the world status quo that was constituted more by American engagement than by any other single element over the last fifty years, then look to see how possible threats could emerge out of that status quo, and then, if they don't find such threats, conclude that U.S. engagement is not needed. But their argument fails to consider how threats would change in the absence of U.S. engagement. Also, it is based entirely on threats and not on opportunities.

Now, the problem I saw in Wohlforth's paper is that it talks about intangible interests and honor as though they were the same thing because it examines only decisions for war. That limitation can be defended in that it creates a manageable body of experience to consider. But it tends to leave out an important reality, which is that for very long periods, Russian foreign policy was identified with higher principles that Russia was advancing or expressing. That's another kind of intangible interest, just as the principles of democracy and the market have been identified with American policy. For those who aren't well versed in Russian history, I'll run through some of these cases.

First, from 1711 to 1800 and then from 1825 to 1914, Russian foreign policy was identified with the defense of Orthodox Christians under Ottoman rule; later it shifted gradually from Orthodox Christians to Orthodox Slavs as the beneficiaries of this policy. Parts of that foreign-policy emphasis were: Catherine the Great's "Greek Project," which went on for a very long time—up to her death—which was to conquer the Balkans, revive the Byzantine Empire under the rule of her grandson (who had been named Constantine for the purpose), and create a kingdom of Dacia in the Balkans for her lover, Potemkin; then, in 1796 the related "Oriental Project," which was the conquest of the Caucasus and Persia as well as the Balkans and Constantinople. It seems to me that the books I've read on Russian foreign policy have not explained very well why these rather proto-Napoleonic projects arose. I just raise that as a question.

For our current discussion, however, I think that the record of Catherine the Great raises an important matter: the problem of hypocrisy in the advocacy of intangible interests in foreign policy. It would be crazy to have a kind of Kantian foreign policy in which everything you do is precisely contrary to your interests. In a way that is what Clinton's first-term policy tried to do, but it never tried seriously and therefore it reversed itself very quickly. The only sensible formula is to try to find a definition of ideals or principles and a definition of interests that on the whole reinforce each other, though they can't do so in every case. Posterity has judged that Catherine, though she had grand humanitarian projects, was a hypocrite. When she partitioned the kingdom of Poland and brought it under Russian rule, her professed concern for the self-determination of Christians was shown to be not totally true. If we want to argue that American foreign policy should have intangible goals among others, we must deal with the problem of hypocrisy.

Paul I at one point in his brief rule (1796-1801) advocated an alliance with Napoleon to annex Constantinople and conquer India—the same kind of idea. Then from 1825 to 1917 Russia generally supported and used as a justification the Balkan Christian independence movements and the sufferings of the Armenians in the Ottoman Empire. I think those policies were sensible, because they made Russia appear more European. They dealt with the problem of Russia as the outsider, which Dr. Wohlforth described quite well, and they also had the useful effect of making Turkey seem less European.

These policies enabled Russia, moreover, to draw upon external resources. That is, in addition to what the Russian army and Russian diplomacy could do, there were all those rebellions in the Balkans, which over time proved to be quite useful. Another example of that was the Russian defense of religious toleration in Poland during the 1760s. As Panin wrote to Prince Repnin, Russia was trying to "create through our co-religionists [that is, the Orthodox population in Poland, plus the Protestants] a firm and reliable party legally entitled to participate in the affairs of Poland." Clever, I believe.

Another point to consider was Russia's interest in European security structures. This was well expressed by a now forgotten analyst of Russian history, Vladimir Weidlé, in 1952: "If there was any constant element in Russia's policy, it was her devotion to the idea of a European system [that's the same as what we mean now by a security structure] to be developed, maintained, and defended against every threat." There were three important phases of that effort. First, there was Paul I's coalition against what he called "philosophical systems that menace order," i.e., the French Revolution, beginning in 1796. Then came Alexander I's coalition against the French in 1801-7, which, as he described it to his representative in Paris, was to set up a kind of U.N. to secure "the sacred rights of humanity, achieve a general pacification, and set up a new code of the law of nations," which would be enforced by collective security. I believe that was crazy; these more cosmic kinds of intangible interests can lead rulers into a sort of craziness.

Then in 1815 this project of Alexander I was renewed in a more reasonable way with the Holy Alliance, which was an agreement by all the powers except Britain—Russia, Austria, and Prussia—to be guided by Christianity and to behave like brothers to one another and like fathers to their peoples. This agreement has been much condemned by liberal historians. But it was a lot more sensible than the hopes of 1801. I think Alexander I had really learned something in the intervening fourteen years because the Holy Alliance was backed up, not by a global collective-security arrangement, but by the Quadruple Alliance of Russia, Prussia, Austria, and Britain to guarantee the Peace of Paris. I think one can defend the suggestion that Metternich's understanding of the Vienna peace settlement suffered from a lack of rhetoric and Alexander I supplied the rhetoric, though it was a little too rich for my tastes. But I think if one can respect the Vienna settlement—and Kissinger's *A World Restored* is a very eloquent argument to that effect—one also has to respect the Holy Alliance.

There was a minor echo of this theme of Russian foreign policy in the Hague Conferences of 1899 (which gave us the International Court of Justice) and 1907. Of course, that theme of humanitarian aims advanced by great-power policy came back with a rush with the Bolshevik Revolution. The Soviet policy of defending dissatisfied classes and groups around the world in the name of world revolution led to some serious mistakes. But as Wohlforth says, "the Soviet Union's status increased in each decade from the 1920s until the 1970s" while until the 1980s "the Western powers were continually on the defensive." In the large this stunning success was attributable to the fact that there are always dissatisfied parties in the international structure, and if you appeal to them in some way you get some support beyond the power of your own country. Contrary to what is normally said, I think it was socialism in one country and the Hitler-Stalin pact that were the bigger mistakes, because they fatally compromised the reputation of the international Communist movement for idealism. The Hitler-Stalin pact, though absolutely justified on realist grounds because the Soviet leaders just couldn't work with Chamberlain and Daladier, was, if you look at the whole strategy of Soviet foreign policy, a catastrophic mistake.

Let me add one footnote on the Soviet period, which is a kind of disagreement with Wohlforth's paper. The Bolsheviks adopted the defense of higher principles in foreign policy, which was a very big element of imperial Russian foreign policy, in a far more extreme form. But they downgraded honor in the narrower sense—that is, how you react to some demeaning demand or how you face up to a situation that tests you. A very important part of Bolshevism was the reaction against many things in traditional Russian culture. In many ways the Bolsheviks really wanted to turn Russians into Germans. They disliked what they saw as the Russian tendency to emotionalism, sentiment, and the emphasis of honor in policy. The great symbol of that was Brest-Litovsk: this absolutely unfair and humiliating peace treaty was greeted by Lenin with open arms. It really split the Bolsheviks from the left Socialist Revolutionaries. Brest-Litovsk, as a symbol of the necessity for a tactical retreat when the correlation of forces is unfavorable, was always an important dimension of Soviet foreign policy. I think it explains why Khrushchev backed down in the Cuban Missile Crisis, when we now know that he was holding the stronger cards. It was also the reason why Gorbachev gave up in Eastern Europe in 1989, with catastrophic effects.

In summary, then, the logic of Dr. Wohlforth's paper is quite brilliant, and while I would have liked to see his historical investigation enlarged, I certainly agree with what he concludes from that investigation: that intangible goals were more important for Russia than other countries because Russia had to fight its way into the great-power club as an outsider from the other side of the tracks.

3

The Politics of Grandeur:
De Gaulle and National Identity

Daniel J. Mahoney

T he concept of "the national interest" is omnipresent in contemporary discussions of foreign affairs—in the speeches of presidents and senators, in the scribblings of editorialists, in the specula-
tions of academic specialists. The influence of this idea is one of
the lasting legacies of the so-called realist school of international
relations during the early Cold War years, whose luminaries included
the political scientist Hans Morgenthau and the theologian Reinhold
Niebuhr. The proponents of "realism" were publicists as well as scholars, who engaged in a polemic against the notion that American foreign policy ought to engage in crusades on behalf of such "abstract"
causes as democracy, human rights, or anti-Communism. Its proponents were "Burkeans," who tried, paradoxically enough, to wish
away the reality of Jacobinism and its ideological pedigree. As Raymond Aron suggested, the American realists transformed the history
of specific periods in European statecraft, such as those between the
Wars of Religion and the French Revolution and between the close

Daniel J. Mahoney is chairman of the Department of Politics at Assump-
tion College, Worcester, Massachusetts. He is the author of *De Gaulle:
Statesmanship, Grandeur and Modern Democracy* (1996) and *The Liberal Political
Science of Raymond Aron* (1992).

of the Napoleonic Wars and the First World War, where the "moderate Machiavellianism" of the European cabinets reigned, into a normative account of the permanently valid requirements of statecraft. Theirs was a conservative, nostalgic, even reactionary lament against the unleashing of societal passions in an age of ideology and mass democracy. Its allure was enhanced by its claim to the considerable "authority" of social science.

Some of today's historically minded realists, such as Henry Kissinger, occasionally concede the historically specific character of their realist prescriptions, but most lament the stubborn persistence of the idea of American "exceptionalism." This is somehow evidence both of the immaturity of the American people and of the utopian imagination of the American political class. But the realists fail to appreciate fully that American exceptionalism is another name for the "universalism" that seems inseparable from American statecraft, because it is integral to America's founding principles and therefore to our very self-definition as a nation.

This is not the occasion to examine the nature of American exceptionalism or its role in the articulation of a distinctively "American" foreign policy. But it is useful to contrast America's universalist principles with those of the European state that also embodies universalist claims or pretensions. I am referring to France, simultaneously the "eldest daughter of the Church" and the originator of what Burke called the "catechism of the rights of man."

The realists are undoubtedly right in saying that American exceptionalism leads some Americans to reject the ways of the world, to consider America too good to muddy itself in the rough-and-tumble of international political life. French universalism, by contrast, does not preclude the French from pursuing their interests, and they are unapologetic about the "Machiavellian" requirements of statecraft. (Witness the cool response of French public opinion to the complicity of their intelligence services and almost certainly President Mitterrand in the bombing of Greenpeace's *Rainbow Warrior* in a New Zealand harbor in 1984.) Many on both the left and the right, Gaullists and socialists alike, continue to believe that France has a distinctive "mission" to perform on behalf of liberty, even though their nation's rank in the world has considerably declined in this century. In this sense, the French remain historically and politically minded in a Europe that is increasingly depoliticized.

(But perhaps this is just a fading ember from the fire lit by General de Gaulle two generations ago.)

It is instructive, therefore, to recognize that this French sensibility, simultaneously universalist and Machiavellian, is distinct from the realism codified by American academic specialists. The American realists despise all ideological pretensions; "power politics," not the cultivation of glory or the defense or promotion of national ideals, is at the center of their political universe. They ignore the manifold and contentious ends of foreign affairs and reduce thinking about the national interest to a question of means: the realistic statesman is chiefly concerned with the calculation of forces and the shifting requirements of the balance of power.[1] American neo-realists, such as Kenneth Waltz, have proudly scientized this already sharply reductive focus; their world is stripped of nations as well as ideologies, history as well as popular passions; international relations becomes a chess-like game played in almost complete independence from the messy contingencies of domestic politics.[2] Such theories dominate the teaching of international relations in the United States, even though it is a country where, in contrast, as Tocqueville tells us, *public opinion* is the sovereign and uncontested ruler of public life and, willy-nilly, of foreign policy itself.[3]

In what follows, I will not try to summarize "French" thinking about foreign policy or the French understanding of the "national interest." Any such attempt would be hopelessly summary and abstract. Instead, I will highlight the thought of Charles de Gaulle, the statesman and political thinker who has most deeply reflected on the meaning of France and its role in the modern world.[4] De Gaulle, with his penetrating recognition of the persistence of national identity, reminds American realists of the necessity and even nobility of reflection on the independence, rank, and grandeur of political communities. In the course of my presentation, I will also refer to a range of important French thinkers—from Alexis de Tocqueville to Raymond Aron—who have addressed de Gaulle's themes, though they have not always provided the same answers to his questions. Finally, I will reflect upon the prospects for self-government and national sovereignty, presupposed and championed by de Gaulle, in a Europe increasingly committed to a supranational project of civil and commercial association lacking in authoritative political direction.

DE GAULLE AS A "REALIST"

If Americans think at all about France today, they do so through the lens of an unexamined prejudice. It is widely held that, of all European states, France has least resigned itself to its diminished place in the world, that it alone maintains a somewhat ridiculous and certainly irrational concern for its "rank" even though it has ceased to be a world power of any consequence. We Americans cannot resist being a bit condescending towards France and its greatest statesman, Charles de Gaulle. He is both admired and dismissed as the noble if irrelevant architect of France's anachronistic and annoying posturings.

Putting all prejudices aside, let us try to articulate the politics of grandeur *as de Gaulle himself understood it*. De Gaulle is commonly perceived as both a "Machiavellian" realist and a starry-eyed romantic. Perhaps this common opinion, in its confusion, provides the best starting point for a presentation of the Gaullist politics of grandeur.

De Gaulle undoubtedly shared certain first principles with the realist school. These include the recognition that the nation-state, as the contemporary embodiment of the political community, is the central unit of international life, and that force remains an indispensable instrument of statecraft. De Gaulle also shares with the realists an untroubled acceptance of the role that duplicity and flexibility inevitably play in diplomatic conduct, as well as a keen appreciation of the balance of power as the means by which order and a kind of sociality are maintained amidst the competitive interplay of sovereign states.

De Gaulle had a broad and deep, perhaps an obsessive, historical memory: he quaintly called East Germany "Prussia" and "Saxony," and he feared the reunification and revival of a centralized "Reich," even a democratic and Western-oriented one.[5] He wisely and nobly promoted France's reconciliation with Adenauer's Germany but did not look forward to a united Germany in *any* form. Despite initial misgivings and hesitations, he supported the North Atlantic Treaty of 1949, partly out of anti-totalitarian conviction but mainly because he feared that the European balance of power was shifting dangerously in favor of a Soviet *imperium*. His rhetoric combined—or oscillated between—a genuine appreciation of the new ideological dimensions of politics in the twentieth century and a dogmatic insistence that what was really at stake in the Cold War was the age-old question of the European balance of power.[6] He clearly recognized the "totalitarian" character of the Soviet-style regimes but was not convinced that the totalitarian or ideological character of the Soviet Union fundamentally affected its pursuit of imperial domination. This partisan of "eternal France" finally saw only "eternal Russians" at work in the machinations of Communism and the movements of the Red Army.[7]

This helps explain why de Gaulle supported an Atlantic Treaty in 1949 but did not hesitate to undermine the ideological solidarity of the Atlantic Alliance after 1965. He unwisely took it for granted that his countrymen would continue to recognize the "totalitarian" character of the Soviet regimes and therefore would accept the necessity of Western solidarity (as de Gaulle himself did, to his credit, during the Cuban Missile Crisis of 1962). This neglect of ideology sometimes led to significant missteps on de Gaulle's part. He wildly overestimated the "national" and "liberal" character of certain post-Stalinist regimes such as Gomułka's or Ceaușescu's (!). He presupposed an American commitment to liberal Europe even as he pursued détente with the East and railed against American "hegemony." One is tempted to conclude that de Gaulle was a realist in the worst sense of the term, sharing the realist school's "unrealistic" neglect of the ideological dimensions of statecraft in our century.

Giving Ideology Its Due

But the truth is, I think, a good deal more complex. To begin with, in his pre-war writings de Gaulle showed a real awareness of the historical specificity of the old regime's non-ideological statecraft.

In his 1938 work *France and Her Army,* de Gaulle expresses his admiration for the *ancien régime,* the classical period of modern history *par excellence.*[8] The statecraft of the old regime reflected a healthy balance between the requirements of self-affirmation and those of measure or moderation. It was a pre-ideological politics and policy of "circumstances" that eschewed abstractions and reflected a taste for the empirical, for concrete facts, and for the requirements of state. The European system of the balance of power established a self-regulating and self-limiting order of nations that rejected "furious ambitions" and "inexpiable hatreds."[9] De Gaulle recognizes that the classical period of French and Europe statecraft came to an end with the ideological wars inaugurated by the French Revolution. He appreciates that the mechanism of the balance of power, which continues to be of permanent validity for political life, is not always or necessarily accompanied by the measured sensibility of the old regime, which aimed to achieve "a just proportion between the end pursued and the forces of the state"[10] and to avoid great national or ideological passions. De Gaulle believed that religious and ideological sectarianism "poison[s] the relations between nations and menace[s] the order of the world."[11]

It is necessary, then, to reconsider our initial judgment about de Gaulle's neglect of the ideological dimensions of modern politics. Perhaps his position is best understood as anti-ideological; his description of the contemporary world is fundamentally prescriptive. As a "domestic" statesman, he wished to heal and transcend France's sectarian and ideological divisions, to overcome the longstanding division between "the Old Regime and the Revolution," between partisans of monarchical France and republican France. He also worked for a transformed European order where great and free and ancient nations would coexist within a common European framework of shared principles and restrained enmities, and he saw an intimation of that future order in the renaissance of national sentiment in Central Europe evident in the Polish and Hungarian uprisings of 1956.

In retrospect, it is clear that de Gaulle overstated the continuities between older national forms and contemporary ideological states. He exaggerated the permanence of such provincial entities as "Prussia" and "Saxony" and seemed to take for granted the solidity and permanence of the nation-state itself. However, unless we recognize the prescriptive character of de Gaulle's account of the forces that move the modern world, unless we see that his relative de-emphasis of ideological considerations reflects a profoundly anti-ideological cast of mind and is itself an element of his statesmanship aiming to bring such a world somewhat closer, we will misunderstand and underestimate him.

DE GAULLE AS A "ROMANTIC"

Like the statesmen of the Old Regime, de Gaulle had a decidedly concrete cast of mind. Whatever the real or superficial resemblances between his thought and that of the American realists, he never transformed the order of nations into a lifeless "system" unconnected to the hopes, beliefs, and passions of real citizens and statesmen.

For de Gaulle, commonly perceived as a realist, also possessed a "romantic" faith in the greatness and rank of France. This concern with the nation's rank is understandable enough: France had suffered a near mortal wound in 1940. De Gaulle did everything within his power to counter the feelings of self-disgust brought on by the Vichy debacle of May-June 1940 and the ensuing armistice. France must "aim high," he said, proudly guarding its rank and reputation and protecting every mark of sovereignty, if it were to recover its independence and self-respect.[12] But de Gaulle was no narrow or quixotic nationalist. He recognized that France's identity was tied to its integration within two larger "wholes" that are, in part, defined by France even as they define France: "Europe" and "civilization." (I will turn to de Gaulle's vision of a "Europe of nations" a little later.)

De Gaulle capaciously shared the universalist self-understandings of both sides of the French ideological divide. He often spoke of France's universal mission, as in this representative line from his *Memoirs of Hope*: from "time immemorial, it had been in [France's] nature to accomplish 'les gestes de Dieu,' to disseminate freedom of thought, to be a champion of humanity."[13]

Because he aimed to rally the French beyond and above ideological divisions, de Gaulle could not simply identify the "mission" of France with the cause of Christendom, with the historic achievements of the Old Regime, or with the Rights of Man and the legacy of the Revolution. His ecumenical "mystique" of France—republican to be sure, but not excluding the old France from its memory or glory—had room for each of these defining moments of French "greatness." Following the poet-philosopher Charles Péguy, de Gaulle believed that "eternal France" could embody a mystique that would counteract the rampant individualism integral to our self-absorbed modern societies. The politics of grandeur aimed to moderate the enervating effects of liberal individualism. In doing so, it drew upon all the "mystiques" of the French past, in order to inspire the self-transcendence necessary to maintain civic life under conditions of modern liberty.[14]

Grandeur and Democratic Life

In a manner reminiscent of Tocqueville, de Gaulle feared the enervation of modern individuals resulting from a private and apolitical understanding of human liberty. We sometimes forget that the sober

Tocqueville, though a friend of democracy, advocated a quasi-"Gaullist" foreign policy to correct what he saw as the inevitable "softening of mores" and weakening of public spirit inherent in democratic life. Like the post-presidential Nixon (who appealed to the thought and example of both men in his final books), Tocqueville and de Gaulle were convinced that a democratic nation must have a mission "beyond peace." In a letter to John Stuart Mill dated March 8, 1841 (which, incidentally, soured their friendship and cooled Mill's admiration for Tocqueville), Tocqueville explained why he did not side with the "peace party" advocating easy accommodation between France and Britain during the Anglo-French crisis of 1840:

> I do not have to tell you, my dear Mill, that the greatest malady that threatens a people organized as we are is the gradual softening of mores, the abasement of the mind, the mediocrity of tastes; that is where the great dangers of the future lie. One cannot let a nation that is democratically constituted like ours and in which the natural vices of the race unfortunately coincide with the natural vices of the social state, one cannot let this nation take up easily the habit of sacrificing what it believes to be its grandeur to its repose, great matters to petty ones; it is not healthy to allow such a nation to believe that its place in the world is smaller, that it is fallen from the level on which its ancestors had put it, but that it must console itself by making railroads and by making prosper in the bosom of this peace, under whatever condition this peace is obtained, the well-being of each private individual. It is necessary that those who march at the head of such a nation should always keep a proud attitude, if they do not wish to allow the level of national mores to fall very low.[15]

Tocqueville, we see, supported a proud and semi-imperial foreign policy in order to correct the soft, humanitarian, materialistic, and apolitical impulses of democratic peoples. Tocqueville believed that all manifestations of greatness in modern times that did not undermine democratic equality and liberties must be highlighted and encouraged. De Gaulle's "politics of grandeur" entails a similar correction or mitigation of the spirit and mores of democracy, without rejecting the justice or necessity of democracy.

De Gaulle's politics of grandeur, therefore, is not an anachronistic or nostalgic effort to revitalize a half-forgotten aristocratic treasure. It is, instead, a self-conscious effort to deal with the problem of democracy, particularly as that problem comes to light in modern France, still torn in his lifetime by the great struggles between left and right engendered by the cataclysm that was the French Revolution.

For de Gaulle as well as for Tocqueville, France was something infinitely more dignified than an abstract, self-interested "unit" in a competitive game for the maximization of power and prestige. France was an eminent representative of a liberal and Christian civilization threatened in our century by the standardization and mechanization of society. This collectivism had reached its fullest expression in National Socialist and Communist totalitarianism, to be sure, but was also far advanced in liberal Europe as well. (See his important speech on "the crisis of civilization" delivered at Oxford, England, on November 25, 1941.[16]) De Gaulle was struck by this paradox: an unchecked individualism inexorably contributes to collectivist politics and movements. A qualified politics of grandeur—eschewing Napoleonic fantasies and imperialist illusions—would fortify the prospects for liberty at home by strengthening the political context within which liberty unfolds.

De Gaulle never concealed the largely instrumental and rhetorical character of his politics of grandeur. In his *Memoirs of Hope* he frankly tells of explaining to Adenauer how the politics of grandeur, in fact, reflects the *weakness* and not the strength of the French nation:

> More than anything else, political independence commensurate with my country's position and aims was essential to its survival in the future. "The French people," I told him, "had for centuries grown accustomed to think of their country as a mastodon of Europe. It was this sense of their greatness and the responsibilities it entailed that preserved their unity, although by nature, ever since the time of the Gauls, they have been inclined to divisions and airy illusions. Now once again circumstances—by which I mean France's salvation at the end of the war, her strong institutions, and the profound upheaval which the world is undergoing—offer them the chance of fulfilling an international mission, without which they would lose interest in themselves and fall into disruption."[17]

The political necessity of grandeur is also stated with great clarity in the famous first paragraph of his *War Memoirs*:

> All my life I had a certain idea of France. This is inspired by sentiment as much as by reason. The emotional side of me naturally

imagines France, like the princes in the fairy stories or the Madonna in the frescoes, as dedicated to an exalted and exceptional destiny. Instinctively I have the feeling that Providence has created her either for complete successes or for exemplary misfortunes. If, in spite of this, mediocrity shows in her acts and deeds, it strikes me as an absurd anomaly, to be imputed to the faults of Frenchmen, not to the genius of the land. But the positive side of my mind also assures me that France is not really herself unless in the front rank; that only vast enterprises are capable of counterbalancing the ferments of dispersal which are inherent in her people; that our country, as it is, surrounded by the others, as they are, must aim high and hold itself straight, on pain of mortal danger, In short, to my mind, France cannot be France without greatness.[18]

De Gaulle's France is called to greatness; it is dedicated to an exalted and exceptional destiny. And as de Gaulle emphasizes in the first chapter of *The Army of the Future* (1934), a commitment to greatness is also a *practical* imperative if France is to compensate for the military and geographical vulnerability of the French hexagon, especially its untenable border in the northeast and the resulting exposure of Paris.[19] But, above all, a commitment to greatness is a moral necessity. Without a statesmanship imbued with a passion for the greatness and rank of France, the country is destined to be undone by its own passionate but unsettled political temperament and afflicted by a series of partisan divisions deeply rooted in its national and revolutionary past.

What Grandeur Means

Grandeur is a concept at the center of de Gaulle's thought and action, but he never explicitly defines it. We must infer its meaning by unpacking the implications and context of his hortatory rhetoric. Stanley Hoffmann is right to observe that grandeur does not entail an ideology because it is "not unalterably tied to any specific policies or forms of power."[20] The commentators agree that grandeur implies France's continued ability to act decisively on the world stage, to display its ambition in the drama of universal history. Grandeur, above all, involves the self-conscious defense of the independence, honor, and rank of the nation.

But this honorable self-regard does not entail the primacy of foreign over domestic policy. Gaullist grandeur thus cultivates an attitude of solicitude for national unity and self-respect, and not the exercise of unlimited imperial ambitions. De Gaulle's willingness to disembark from Algeria, to the consternation of the partisans of a French Algeria, illustrates that a politics of grandeur is not essentially tied to an imperial option. The concern for rank is, first and foremost, a means toward national flourishing and not an end in itself. It is an indispensable precondition for sustaining the moral and political unity of France. But neither does de Gaulle make foreign policy merely instrumental to domestic concerns. Rather, he affirms the mutual dependence of unity and moderation at home and qualified self-assertion abroad. Unity is a precondition of grandeur, but grandeur makes possible national coherence and flourishing.

De Gaulle believed that only a politics of grandeur could unite the French people around a mystique capable of incorporating and transcending the great division between left and right opened up by the French Revolution. François Furet has argued that de Gaulle created the first widely accepted and fully legitimate regime of post-revolutionary France, the first "republic of the center."[21] I believe that this was de Gaulle's self-conscious intention as a national "legislator." A merely institutional solution to France's problems, one content to restore energy to the executive and to end the domination of parliamentary deputies, could not long sustain the imagination or civic faith of the French people. It risked establishing what Philippe Bénéton has called "consensus without vision."

As we have seen, democratic modernity is characterized by a relentless depoliticization of society. The salutary triumph of commerce and culture, what the philosophers of the eighteenth century called "civilization" or "civil society," paradoxically risks attenuating the civic realm where a common good is articulated through legislative deliberation and, above all (de Gaulle believed), by the executive's actions on behalf of the nation's place in the world. What contemporary American conservatives wish to do by strengthening the art of association and the vitality of local self-government—namely, to "repoliticize" apathetic and dependent individuals—de Gaulle aimed to do principally through a politics of grandeur.

In addition, de Gaulle also recognized the need for domestic reforms in his highly centralized nation, in order to accomplish this aim of repoliticizing the people. He wished to encourage greater grass-roots participation in the management of business enterprises and proposed the "regionalization" of the senate. His critics are undoubtedly correct in saying that the establishment of a strong, perhaps "hyper-presidential" republic in France after 1958 was in some tension with his desire to reinvigorate French civil society. His highly centralized Fifth Republic made politics inaccessible to ordinary citizens except through the most distant forms of representation. His emphasis on grandeur was also substantially at odds with the commercial and utilitarian character of modern life. But the refounding of the French state was necessary to correct the weakness of the previous parliamentary republic, to overcome its ideological divisions, and to restore France's place in the world. Anglo-American commentators sometimes forget that there can be no civil society without a political instrument to forge and protect it.

DE GAULLE AND EUROPEAN UNITY

Whatever the problems with his specific solutions or recommendations, de Gaulle wanted, above all, to preserve political life, at least in its national form. And he saw a transnational "Europe," in its dominant expression, as a threat to the preservation of a properly political existence. But, someone might retort, must one choose between "Europe" and political life? Doesn't the European project, the building of a united Europe, provide an adequate substitute for national self-assertion? Isn't "Europe" capable of providing an ennobling substitute for the older forms of political life?

That is certainly the shared faith (or illusion) of the dominant part of the French and European political elite today. In 1993, the French government even went so far as to claim de Gaulle for the cause of transnational Europe, by putting up billboards and signs announcing that Charlemagne, Napoleon, and de Gaulle would unequivocally recommend a *oui* vote in the French referendum on the Maastricht Treaty! De Gaulle, of course, was a "good European," and he played an important role in advancing Franco-German reconciliation and in cementing European union after 1958. But the contemporary European political class hesitates between the "transnationalist" model of Jean Monnet and Robert Schuman and de Gaulle's confederal model of European unity. Everywhere we are told that "Europe" is inevitable, despite the fact that the relationship of the emerging Europe to the "sovereign" nation-states remains almost wholly unclarified. Pierre Manent has forcefully highlighted this contradiction:

> After the Second World War the European idea and its accompanying institutions facilitated the reconstruction on solid foundations of the European nation-state, while also making plausible, imaginable, and even desirable the withering away of this political form. But does "Europe" today signify the depoliticization of the life of peoples, that is, the increasingly methodical reduction of their collective existence to the activities of civil society and the mechanism of civilization? Or does it instead entail the construction of a new political body, the body of a great, enormous Nation? The construction of Europe has made progress only because of this ambiguity and thus has taken on—as the vector of these two contradictory projects—its character as an imperious, indefinite and opaque movement. Yet this at first rather fortunate ambiguity has become paralyzing and soon risks becoming fatal. The sleepwalker's assurance with which "Europe" pursues its indefinite extension is the result of its refusal to think about itself comprehensively, that is, to define itself politically.[22]

Charles de Gaulle did not share this paralyzing ambivalence. He had a clear vision of a Europe of nations. After returning to power in 1958, he affirmed his government's support for the Treaty of Rome, which established the European Economic Community, and for the process of greater European integration and cooperation. His government was most immediately concerned with rectifying a series of practical economic difficulties, from the maintenance of external tariffs that aimed to sharply differentiate those within the Community from those without, to the establishment of an agricultural policy whose immediate goal was to protect French agriculture from the effects of foreign competition. But de Gaulle's main aims were eminently *political*. He wished to give the new community a specific political identity and to separate it from the larger Atlantic community that was under American direction or domination.

De Gaulle would not be deterred for a moment by the arguments of free-market economists in favor of the abundant economic advantages of free trade. His goal was to prevent France from becoming an instrument of a larger movement of global standardization and depoliticization, whatever the strictly "economic" rationale accompanying that process. He would not allow Britain to enter the Community because

Britain's special relationship with the United States and its continuing ties with its dominions and Commonwealth prevented it from giving itself wholeheartedly to "Europe" as a cohesive political configuration. The British, on the contrary, wanted to be a member of the Community while also maintaining their special relationship with the Commonwealth and their existing free-trade agreements. Despite the needlessly provocative rhetoric justifying de Gaulle's vetoes of British membership in the Community, one should recognize that he was essentially correct in arguing that Britain's ambivalence about its European identity would have prevented any effective movement toward a coherent, political Europe.

A Europe of Nations

Let us return to the question: What kind of political Europe should Europe aim to establish, according to de Gaulle? In his *Memoirs of Hope,* he states that "having no taste for make-believe" he rejected "the hopes and illusions of the supra-national school."[23] De Gaulle had no faith in a "federation without a federator." An administrative apparatus, such as the Brussels commission that administers the affairs of the European Community, could not provide architectonic political direction for Europe. De Gaulle believed that such direction could come only from the coordinated activities of *states*. He thought that each European state must preserve its distinct "national personality" while coordinating activities in the diplomatic, military, economic, and cultural spheres. He accepted "the technical value of certain more or less extra-national or supra-national organisms" but believed that these must be instruments of the common action of nation-states, the essential "pillars" of a united Europe.[24]

There is no doubt that de Gaulle desired French leadership for his Europe of nations. He also wished to hedge Germany in by tying it to a larger whole that would circumscribe its actions. He saw leadership of this community of nations as a means by which France could approximate its previous rank, even if it were no longer anything like the "mastodon" of old. De Gaulle would, undoubtedly, have had grave concerns about German reunification and would have been surprised and troubled by the fact that France has even less independence and room for maneuver after the decline of the dual "hegemony" of the superpowers than it had during the Cold War. (But unlike Mitterrand, who acknowledged the "progressive" if flawed character of the Communist regimes in the East and deplored resurgent nationalism,[25] de Gaulle almost certainly would have *welcomed* the collapse of Communist ideology and would have accepted the reassertion of national identities in "the other Europe.")

Today, however, it is commonplace to dismiss de Gaulle's European vision as anachronistic. Political scientists proclaim the death of "high politics" and welcome the globalization of culture and the economy. Political theorists such as Jürgen Habermas announce the necessity of a new European citizenship, based upon the requirements of "procedural rationality," which will transcend the particularity of the nation-state.[26] The American philosopher Martha Nussbaum insists that we are witnessing the emergence of a new global consciousness and identity, a patriotism rooted in the very humanity of man, and she claims the authority of classical philosophy for these extravagant hopes![27]

Perhaps, then, de Gaulle is the realist after all. He did help initiate the one concrete "European act" that did more than anything else to put an end to the cycle of European wars and recriminations: the reconciliation of France and Germany.[28] In grand Gaullist fashion, he arranged to have this rapprochement solemnly ratified by a requiem mass at Rheims in 1962 attended by himself and Konrad Adenauer. It was his grand hope that Europe would act as a cohesive entity in the world, particularly in matters of defense and foreign policy. In contrast, the present European Community incessantly proclaims the desirability of such coordination but obstinately resists the implementation of any effective policy worthy of a political Europe.

The great French political philosopher Raymond Aron was both a strong supporter of the Atlantic Alliance and a sometime target of the wrath of de Gaulle because of his refusal to toe a Gaullist line. More of a liberal than de Gaulle, he believed that a grandiloquent rhetoric of grandeur was misplaced in modern circumstances and could not resist the inevitable "disenchantment" of political life. Yet Aron agreed with de Gaulle that the nation-state was the only viable political instrument available today, and he too rejected the utopian fantasies of intellectuals who heralded a non-existent "multinational citizenship." To be sure, a global industrial or post-industrial "society" was forming as a result of the commercial and cultural ties connecting hitherto separated peoples. "Universal history" was dawning as a reality.[29] But there was no evidence that "society" in any form could replace the necessities of *political* deliberation and *political* self-definition obliging even democratic peoples. As Pierre Manent has suggested in a quite parallel way, while one "can readily admit that one can renounce the nation as a political form, I do not believe that peoples can live long within civilization alone without some sense of political belonging (which is necessarily exclusive), and thus without some definition of what is held in common."[30] Despite the claims of its partisans, there is far too little evidence that a political Europe can provide that sense of belonging or articulate a coherent understanding of shared political purposes.

Europe was terribly scarred and perhaps permanently dispirited by the wars that marked the first part of the twentieth century. Its peoples are exhausted, and its political elites shirk the obligation to think and act politically. Twenty years ago, in the concluding chapter of his magisterial *Clausewitz* ("A Farewell to Arms, or the Great Illusion"), Aron wrote that

> the great illusion of today is not that which threw the people of Europe into suicidal opposition; it is the contrary illusion, that of the Europeans and sometimes even the Americans, which ascribes a single rationality to all peoples and to those who govern them, namely that of the economists who compare cost and effect. The Europeans would like to leave behind history with a capital H, which writes its letters in blood.[31]

The intervening acceleration of the European project has done nothing to alter the accuracy of Aron's judgment.

In the preface to his 1932 book *The Edge of the Sword*, de Gaulle presciently warned against the illusion that society could proceed apace without authoritative political direction and without a willingness to use its military instruments in defense of its political ends.[32] Today, in contrast, Europeans act as if they share Marx's confidence that the "administration of things" is inevitably replacing the government of men. They act as if Europe, happily or fortunately without Machiavellian statecraft and content with its post-historical state, once again prefigures the universal destiny of mankind.

Today many dismiss de Gaulle's concerns as noble but finally romantic and therefore anachronistic. It is undoubtedly true that de Gaulle acutely *felt* the decline of the older Europe that he knew and loved and tried to reinvigorate through his politics of grandeur. In

Felled Oaks, André Malraux reproduces de Gaulle's haunting lament, at the end of his life, about the failure of his project to revitalize France and Europe:

> France was the soul of Christianity—today, let us say, the soul of European civilization. I did all I could to restore her. . . . Good luck to this federation without a federator! . . . You know as well as I do that Europe will be a compact among the States, or nothing. Therefore, nothing. We are the last Europeans in Europe, which was Christianity. A tattered Europe, but it did exist. The Europe whose nations hated one another had more reality than the Europe of today. It is no longer a matter of wondering whether France will make Europe, it is a matter of understanding that she is threatened with death through the death of Europe.[33]

The dark, brooding tone of de Gaulle's lament can be attributed, in some part, to his belief that France had broken its "contract" with him in April 1969 by defeating a referendum he had put forward, ostensibly to reform the organization of the French senate but with a larger purpose of renewing his mandate from the people. Whatever the idiosyncrasies of de Gaulle's notion of political legitimacy, this so-called romantic had perfectly grasped the fundamental contradiction at the heart of the contemporary European project, as well as the profound depoliticization that accompanies the triumph of democracy in the Western world. The fact that such sober thinkers as Tocqueville and Aron echo some of de Gaulle's deepest concerns suggests that his insights ultimately transcend the idiom in which they were expressed, as well as some of the policies to which they give rise.

A Response

Francis Fukuyama

Professor Mahoney's excellent paper can serve as a valuable antidote to American academic realism in international relations. It's a good reminder that there are real countries out there whose behavior simply cannot be understood in terms of the realists' formal models. A lot of the debate in recent years has been between the billiard-ball realists and the people who think that ideology—e.g., liberalism—is important. Mahoney reminds us that there is a third category, which is the nation-state, understood not in ideological terms but more in Burkean terms as a historical community that is grounded in certain traditions, each one of which leads to a different definition of national interest. International relations has to take account of those traditions.

However, I have some problems with the celebration of de Gaulle and the French foreign policy from the Gaullist period on. It seems to me that it's a defective foreign policy because it arises from a defective political system.

First of all, Gaullist foreign policy is really a product of the Gaullist state. It can arise only in a highly centralized, bureaucratized, state-centered republic. It is not characteristic of French foreign policy

Francis Fukuyama is Hirst Professor of Public Policy at the Institute of Public Policy at George Mason University. He is the author of *The End of History and the Last Man*.

across the board. In fact, it seems to me that only in certain periods of French history, when France moved from the Fourth Republic model to the Fifth Republic model, could France have a Gaullist foreign policy. That is to say, French history, ever since the Revolution, has alternated between extremely weak parliamentarism and a kind of hyper-presidentialism. None of the earlier republics—First, Second, Third, and especially the Fourth Republic—was able to run anything remotely like a Gaullist foreign policy because they all had a very weak executive, a weak coalition government.

The reason de Gaulle came back to power in 1958 was that the Fourth Republic couldn't solve the problem of Algeria. There was no question of grandeur or the lack of it: they simply couldn't cope with Algeria. In order to deal with a crisis of state weakness, the French go to the other extreme of creating an either outright authoritarian or hyper-presidential system of government. A Gaullist foreign policy cannot be run in anything other than a Gaullist, strongly presidential, constitutional system.

Professor Mahoney mentioned the *Rainbow Warrior* case, where the French intelligence agencies had been fooling around with the Greenpeace activists. French foreign policy is full of cases like that; there is no parliamentary scrutiny, no press scrutiny. The French were heavily involved with the machinations in Rwanda that led to the current problem in that part of the world; they were running a kind of unaccountable and in many ways highly cynical foreign policy, completely free of any scrutiny of the kind that would occur in a less presidential, more participatory form of democracy. The real reason for this is the weakness of civil society in France, which is also the central issue analyzed by de Tocqueville.

The reason that the French have alternated between weak parliamentarism and hyper-presidentialism is that they have never found this kind of Anglo-Saxon balance where you can have strong institutions, political parties, corporations, and the like between the individual or family and the state; these allow society to be in some sense self-organizing, and that gives citizenship a place that is not centered on the state itself. If you compare the French system to the American, you see that it's a totally different kettle of fish. This explains a great deal of the difference in foreign policies.

From the beginning, the United States has been characterized by, on the one hand, a weak state, by federalism, by weak political parties, by a separation of powers and a great division of political authority, and on the other hand, by a strong civil society, a powerful corporate private sector, strong NGOs, and strong private associations across the board. This has made it possible for American society to be cohesive and very dynamic in the absence of a strong executive. As a result, for most of America's history, foreign policy has been weak to non-existent.

There are good reasons, built into the political system, why isolationism has been a powerful trend. I think the post-war period is an exception, where the growth of a large welfare state at home was matched by the rise of a large national-security state in order to meet the Soviet challenge. But that's not necessarily a disproof of American exceptionalism, because Americans had to operate in typically American ways to build a consensus for a strong international role based on a high degree of moralism and universalism—getting the Truman Doctrine and the Marshall Plan and support for NATO and the like.

My prediction is that a lot of that is going to vanish. You can already see it slipping away in the post–Cold War world. I think we'll probably go back to the more normal pattern (I'm not saying that this is desirable, but only that it's likely) where, as the United States proceeds in deconstructing its welfare state and its strong centralized government, this will lead to the deconstruction in its foreign policy of a strong international role.

There's also a cultural difference between France and the United States just in the matter of Protestant and Catholic morality. The French family is much more stable than the American family, but French men always have mistresses on the side. There is a counterpart in French foreign policy: there is an abiding long-term principle, but in the short run, the French are perfectly willing to sell out friends and enemies in cynical ways that would not be possible in a northern European Calvinist society. I think that these two political systems are fundamentally incompatible and that their solutions to problems of community and citizenship are really quite different.

The thing in Professor Mahoney's paper that I strongly disagreed with was this statement: "What contemporary American conservatives wish to do by strengthening the art of association and the vitality of local self-government—namely, to repoliticize apathetic and dependent individuals—de Gaulle aimed to do principally through a politics of grandeur." Those are really quite different agendas, in my opinion. It may be that some American conservatives believe strengthening the family and civil society is a means of strengthening civic virtue and the American state, but for the most part the people who want a strong civil society want a weak national government. They want a strong family and strong charitable associations because they want to pull back the welfare state and to off-load a lot of its responsibilities onto civil society, where they believe such responsibilities belong. In France the problem has always been different. There has not been a strong civil society, and so the alternatives are almost cast in terms of the individual and the family on the one side and the state on the other. It's natural in a French context, then, that politicizing people and strengthening the idea of civic responsibility necessarily results in a strong state, and in citizenship understood as participation in a share of government and the state. To confuse the Gaullist alternative with the agenda of American conservatives is not right.

Which is more realistic? Leaving aside the question of which is better in normative terms, I think the French model has a lot of problems, especially in view of the way the global economy has developed. It is very difficult to have that kind of nation-state–centered political volunteerism. However nice it might be in normative terms to have citizenship defined that way, in the modern world it leads to a lot of problems. We see an example in the French state's attempts to ban the Internet, and when French commissioners in the European Community try to regulate all sorts of markets. In the long run, I think, such actions are going to lead to a kind of economic disaster for France.

I agree completely with Mahoney on the Gaullist critique of the European Union. I think that what is currently being put forward in the Maastricht Treaty and the proposed European Monetary Union is a highly depoliticized vision of what Europe ought to be. It is a Europe built by technocrats, and for that reason it simply will not work. No political European identity is being created, and Professor Mahoney is right in arguing that the Gaullist critique is going to prove to be decisive. On the other hand, it seems to me the real threat to the nation-state is not from supranational entities like the EU but from smaller subnational kinds of identities, or multinational corporations, or transnational NGOs, or ethnicity. A lot of other sources of political identity are competing besides the nation-state; in fact, the nation-state looks like a fairly weak force.

Finally, while I can understand this vision of grandeur and the nation as being an antidote for the depoliticizing effects of modern commercialism and the privatization of modern life, it's not really clear that it will be an adequate antidote, for a couple of reasons. First of all, the whole Hegelian notion that you need a national political community because ultimately it can make war and that you can have citizenship grounded in war and so forth—that nice little wars like the Franco-Prussian War would be good for the domestic political system because they would remind people of what heroism and sacrifice were—this was conceivable, though barely, in the nineteenth century. But that's just not the world we're living in now. That kind of politics, that understanding of history as mainly driven by national interests and the competition for power among nation-states, is just too dangerous in the modern world.

Realistically, I think that during the next two centuries the country that has the greatest chance of following a politics of grandeur is the one whose domestic political system will, I predict, most resemble the French system—that is, a weak civil society and a long-term alternation between extremely weak parliamentarism and a kind of a hyper-presidentialism. That country is Russia. Sure enough, that society is now preoccupied with questions of grandeur and rank, of its place in Europe, its historical role protecting Orthodoxy, its conception of the national interest. That is a dangerous situation. We're living in a different kind of world, with different armaments and different stakes, than the world Hegel saw.

A strong foreign policy based on global intervention is not a likely solution for the internal problem of citizenship today. Modern states are so large and impersonal and powerful that it's rather like saying that the solution to depoliticized individualism is a big welfare state. For the reason that *that* is not a satisfactory answer, I am unsure that a politics of grandeur is a realistic solution in a country like the United States, particularly for the problems of excessive individualism and privatization.

4

Alexander Hamilton on Honor and American Foreign Policy

Karl Walling

What do we mean by "national honor"? Do we mean pride? Respectability? National greatness? Self-respect? Self-restraint? Self-assertion? The keeping of promises? Certainly all of these, and perhaps other concepts as well. But since we must begin somewhere, let us define America's national honor provisionally as the correspondence between the claims we make in world affairs and our capacity to uphold them. This definition requires that American deeds be as good as American words. It requires statesmen either to develop the will and the capability to back up their words with deeds, or to scale back their words to match likely deeds, or both. If the American Founders can offer us any guidance for conducting an honorable foreign policy, it must therefore arise from their efforts to balance words and deeds.

Naturally, the Founders did not always agree. Nor were they equally gifted in all things political. Some, like James Madison, were

Karl Walling is John M. Olin Faculty Fellow in History and Political Philosophy at Colorado College. A revised edition of his book *Republican Empire: War and Free Government in the Political Thought of Alexander Hamilton* will be published by University Press of Kansas. He wishes to thank David Hendrickson and Robert Kagan for comments that helped him clarify his thoughts in this essay.

best suited to drafting constitutions and organizing political parties. Others, like Thomas Jefferson, were best at expressing the fundamental principles of our regime. Still others, like Alexander Hamilton, wrote quite frequently and thoughtfully about honor and foreign policy. Hamilton even died in a duel of honor. His life and career exhibit the stakes involved in taking honor seriously.

Hamilton is also the only Founder whose vision of national greatness could rival those of Pericles and Charles de Gaulle, about whom two other contributors to this symposium have spoken. Indeed, Hamilton once wrote under the pseudonym Pericles, revealing his hope that the United States would surpass Periclean Athens.[1] For these reasons, while considering other Founders' views of national honor, this essay will concentrate on Hamilton's view and its implications for contemporary American foreign policy.

THE CONSTITUTION AND NATIONAL HONOR

The prerequisite of an honorable American foreign policy in the Founding era was a new constitution.[2] In 1776, Congress declared that the United States was an independent nation, with a right to wage war, form alliances, and conclude peace. Yet the United States as a confederation of states was not like any other independent nation of its time. On paper in the Articles of Confederation, Congress was vested with *external sovereignty*, or what John Locke called the federative power over foreign affairs. *Internal sovereignty*, however, remained very much with the states, and this gave them de facto control over the executive power of the union as well.[3] No measures of Congress could be enforced without the cooperation of the states. Thus, for example, Congress often requisitioned money from the states to fund the war against England, but the states frequently failed to comply. The very structure of the union made it difficult for Congress to direct the war and vindicate the honor of the United States as an independent nation.[4]

Although the Continental Congress deserves much credit for ultimately winning the War for Independence in the face of the structural limitations of the confederation, American independence probably could not have been won without significant amounts of foreign aid, especially from France. This dependence on foreign aid also called American political independence into question. Even after the war was won, American weakness made many Americans blush for American honor. Listen to the words of Alexander Hamilton as he surveyed America's moral-strategic situation in 1787:

> We may indeed with propriety be said to have reached the last stage of national humiliation. There is scarcely anything that can wound the pride or degrade the character of an independent nation, which we do not experience. . . . Have we valuable territories and important posts [in the Northwest territories] in the possession of a foreign power [Great Britain], which by express stipulations [in the Treaty of Paris] ought long since to have been surrendered? These are still retained, to the prejudice of our interests no less than our rights. Are we in a position to resent or repel the aggression? We have neither troops nor treasury nor government. Are we even in a position to remonstrate with dignity? The just imputations on our own faith, with respect to the same treaty ought first to be removed. . . . Is respectability in the eyes of foreign powers a safeguard against foreign encroachments? The imbecility [weakness] of our government forbids them to treat with us: our ambassadors abroad are the mere pageants of mimic sovereignty.[5]

Hamilton called his readers' attention to two ways in which American deeds failed to match American words. First, the United States was able neither to deter nor to defeat current or future adversaries. Second, the United States lacked the power to live up to its agreements with other nations. The Treaty of Paris required Americans to pay back pre-war debts to British creditors, and to compensate Loyalists for property confiscated during the American Revolution. Although Congress passed the treaty, enforcement remained with the states, which often did little to uphold it and even violated it openly. Under international law, failure to enforce the treaty was a solid justification for war. It also gave the British an excuse for continuing to occupy American territory.

For John Jay, the former secretary of foreign affairs for the Continental Congress and the future first chief justice of the Supreme Court, the Constitution of 1787 was an important means of salvaging American national honor. Jay was especially worried that national weakness might invite or provoke wars with foreign powers in North America, such as Spain and England. To avoid provoking wars, Americans had to abide by their treaty obligations, comply with international law, and refrain from invading the territories of other nations. Yet several state governments had already provoked wars with Indian tribes, and there were always rumors that frontiersmen would try to seize New Orleans from Spain.

As Nathan Tarcov first observed, Jay's efforts to address these problems led him to anticipate Madison's famous argument in *Federalist* 10. Yet quite surprisingly, Jay applied arguments in favor of representation and diversity to foreign rather than domestic policy.[6] Jay argued that a national government would be less prone to faction and better led than the state governments. It would therefore be less likely to violate the rights of other nations deliberately. If the new government were more just, American foreign policy would be more honorable, and the United States would be safer from war with foreign powers as a result. Jay and Hamilton also suggested that the Constitution would enable the courts to apply national treaties against the states. Though we today rarely understand the judiciary as an instrument of American foreign and national security policy, Hamilton and the first chief justice believed the courts could play an important role in securing peace by enabling the national government to honor its treaty obligations.[7]

The Need to Deter

Preventing Americans from provoking wars was not the end of Jay's discussion of national honor and the Constitution, however. He also told the story of the tiny state of Genoa in 1685. Having offended Louis XIV, the Genoans endeavored to appease him. Louis demanded that Genoa send its chief magistrate (the doge) accompanied by a delegation of senators to beg his pardon, and the Genoans were obliged to submit to these terms for the sake of peace. Jay concluded the story by asking whether Louis would have demanded or received a "like humiliation from Spain, or Britain, or any other *powerful* nation."[8]

The moral of Jay's story appears to be that if Americans did not wish to choose between war and national humiliation, they would have to develop a very credible deterrence posture.[9] American justice was not sufficient security against war, and American injustice might even cause war. Regardless of whether Americans were right or wrong in time of war or near war, their first line of defense had to be an energetic, well-constructed union.

Hamilton later revealed the full constitutional and strategic implications of Jay's argument for union as a means to deter war, when possible, and wage it effectively, when necessary. The union had to become a great maritime empire, which could eventually rival even the English empire. Decades before Clausewitz, Hamilton, who had served on General Washington's staff through most of the War for Independence, conceived the possibility of a total, unlimited war in which nations would mobilize every available resource to avoid defeat. In such cases, Congress would need the constitutional authority to raise unlimited amounts of money and numbers of soldiers for the common defense. The executive would require the authority to deploy the nation's troops and resources with firmness and dispatch. With such institutions, it would then be less necessary to choose between war and national humiliation. American power might even become equal to the sometimes unlimited demands of modern warfare.[10]

For many, this was precisely what was wrong with the Constitution of 1787: a government strong enough to confront all the potential demands of war might become unlimited in its powers and unresponsive to popular control. The opponents of the Constitution, the Anti-Federalists, also worried that too much talk about national honor might lead Americans to worship the golden calf of glory. The Anti-Federalist "Brutus" observed that "European governments are almost all of them framed, and administered, with a view to arms, and war, as that in which their chief glory consists; they mistake the end of government: it was designed to save men's lives, not destroy them." Brutus argued that "we ought to furnish the world with the example of a great people, who in their civil institutions hold chiefly in view the attainment of virtue and domestic happiness among themselves. Let the monarchs of Europe share among them the glory of depopulating countries. . . . I envy them not the honor, and I pray this country will never be ambitious for it."[11]

Rights, Not Honor

Virtually every Founder agreed with Brutus on this point: the end of American government is to secure rights, not to compete for honor and glory in martial conflicts with other nations. Thus the American Founding as a whole could be understood as part of the general Enlightenment project to limit or debunk considerations of honor in both foreign and domestic policy. The aim was to weaken older mores and institutions that served human pride in favor of newer ones that secured equal liberty instead.[12] America's most appropriate role in the world was to serve as an exemplary republic, a model of free government for those who had the courage and opportunity to emulate it. This role then became both an object and a standard of national honor: an object, because it helped define the purpose of the new nation; a standard, because it resulted in an American transvaluation of European values.[13] Brutus, for example, did not reject honor as a goal of foreign policy; instead, he redefined honor in terms consistent with universal natural rights. He wanted to ensure that his country practiced what it preached in the Declaration of Independence, a moral ambition that continues to have significant resonance in foreign policy. Since the Founding era at least, arguments for national self-restraint have played at least as much a role in debates over national honor and American foreign policy as those in favor of national self-assertion.

While almost all the Founders shared the moral ambition of Brutus, they did not always agree about the means to pursue it. Some worried that it would be impossible to secure American rights without being much more assertive about American honor than Brutus implied would be necessary. At the Federal Convention, for example, Hamilton criticized the view that "respectability in the eyes of foreign nations" was not a proper object of American government, and that the only object worth considering was "domestic happiness and tranquillity." This, Hamilton observed, was "an ideal distinction. No government could give us tranquillity and happiness at home which did not give us sufficient stability and strength to make us respectable abroad."[14] National honor had to be an important end of foreign policy, not because it was desirable for its own sake, but because it was necessary to the peaceful enjoyment of American rights at home.

Respectability abroad was in fact one important element in James Madison's defense of the United States Senate. Americans needed one branch of government responsible for upholding the national character in relations with other countries, so that American politics would at least "appear to be the offspring of a wise and honorable policy." The Senate's potential "sensibility to the opinion of the world, which is perhaps not less necessary in order to merit, than it is to obtain its respect and confidence," might enable the foreign opinion to function as something like a conscience for the United States. In this way, Madison extended his famous theory of an extended republic to an entire world. World opinion would help check factious tendencies in our foreign policies.[15]

Some Founders went much further than Madison. The most ambitious among them considered it both possible and desirable for the United States to become not merely a respectable nation but also a great one. In keeping with our peculiar national character, however, the pursuit of national greatness had to be expressed in egalitarian terms. For example, Hamilton saw the world divided into four regions in 1787: Europe, Asia, Africa, and America. Unfortunately for the other three, Europe, by arms and by negotiations, by force and by fraud, had acquired dominion over them all and had "come to consider the rest of mankind as created for her benefit." Men admired as profound philosophers in Europe had ascribed Europe's dominion to the physical superiority of its inhabitants. They had even asserted that all animals, including the human species, degenerated in America, that "even dogs cease to bark" after breathing the American atmosphere![16]

In a calculated appeal to Americans' wounded national honor, Hamilton admitted that "facts have too long supported the arrogant pretensions" of the Europeans. It now belonged to the United States to "vindicate the honor" not simply of Americans but "of the human race" by teaching the Europeans a lesson in egalitarian moderation. To do so, the upstart republic needed to aim at an ascendant in the "system of American affairs." This system would begin with the union of the thirteen states, but Hamilton implied it might well extend beyond them and include much of Latin America as well. Anticipating the division of the world into two hemispheres in the Monroe Doctrine, Hamilton's system seemed to require the United States to become something highly paradoxical: an anti–imperial empire "superior to the control of all transatlantic force and influence, and able to dictate the terms of the connection between the old and the new world."[17] In Hamilton's view, all that was necessary to transform this vision of national greatness into reality was a patient policy of staying out of major wars with great powers until the new union had developed its enormous but still latent strength.

TREATY OBLIGATIONS AND NATIONAL HONOR

Unfortunately, this grand strategy was in substantial tension with American treaty obligations in the 1790s, and quarrels over those obligations led to the first great debate over American national honor among the Founders. During the War for Independence, the United States had signed a mutual defense agreement with France. It was supposed to last in "perpetuity"—that is, forever. When war broke out in Europe between revolutionary France on the one hand and Austria and Prussia on the other, President Washington had to decide whether and to what extent the treaty obliged the United States to side with France in a world war that, practically speaking, lasted from Washington's first term until well into the second term of James Madison.

The revolution in France made Washington's decision extremely difficult. Was America bound to France or Louis XVI? Washington's secretary of state, Thomas Jefferson, and the Speaker of the House of Representatives, James Madison, argued that the Franco-American treaty bound the American and French nations, not simply their governments. Therefore, they believed the treaty remained in full force. They also suggested that gratitude to France for aid during the American Revolution, as well as shared republican prejudices in America and France, imposed some additional undefined obligations of honor toward France in American foreign policy. Though neither Jefferson nor Madison advocated entering the war on the side of France, both clearly wanted the United States to tilt toward France in a manner that Hamilton believed was likely to lead to war.[18]

As the first secretary of the treasury and the *de facto* prime minister of the Washington administration, Hamilton believed that strict neutrality was the best policy during this war because the United States' claim to be an independent nation still outstripped its capacity to defend itself. Moreover, rather than attempt to set a price on American neutrality, as advocated by Jefferson in order to gain influence in England and France, Hamilton preferred to state America's neutral position openly and candidly. Playing both ends against the middle ran the risk that the United States would be caught in the growing struggle between these great powers, and might even have to break a promise to one of them.[19] Hamilton's great problem was to find a way to distance the United States from France without violating the treaty commitment.

Hamilton's Defense of Neutrality

Hamilton's complicated defense of Washington's Neutrality Proclamation is instructive, because it reveals many of the dangers of a dogmatic conception of national honor in foreign policy. He agreed
with Jefferson and Madison that, all other things being equal, a revolution in one country does not dissolve another country's treaty
obligations toward it. But while every nation has a right to alter or
abolish its form of government, no nation has a right to involve others
"absolutely and unconditionally" in the consequences of its revolution. A revolutionary government might forfeit the good faith of its
allies if it became so aggressive that it united other major powers
against it. If this possibility of forfeiture did not exist, a government
would have "not only a power over its own happiness, but a power
over the happiness of other" nations as well. The treaty could not be
intepreted as a one-sided obligation for the United States to follow
France down its road to self-destruction as it waged war with all of
Europe.[20]

In order to carve out the maximum possible freedom of maneuver
for the United States, Hamilton also noted some important practical
limits to the duty to honor treaty obligations. Treaties bind only so far
as it is possible for their parties to perform them. France was engaged
in a great land struggle with all of Europe, but the United States was
neither a land nor a naval power. The United States could therefore
do nothing significant to aid France in this war. Moreover, under
Hamilton's reading of international law, treaties do not bind if their
performance becomes suicidal for their parties. Siding with France
risked the possibility that the English navy would sweep American
commerce from the seas. This not only would have devastated American trade but also would have undermined Hamilton's efforts to
restore the honor of American credit and the fiscal solvency of the
United States, which depended on tariffs from British imports.

The disproportion between the services the United States could
render and the harm it might receive if it entered the war was so great
that Hamilton saw ample reason to annul or suspend the French
treaty. If that was not possible, he wished to limit American aid to a
strict performance of precisely stated obligations. The treaty was a
defensive alliance, and technically, France had begun the war in Europe
by attacking Austria and Prussia. Hamilton therefore did not believe

the United States had any obligation to enter the war. Instead, it was free to consult its own interests, which were to stay out of the war for as long as possible.[21]

In contrast, Jefferson argued that unless national survival was immediately at stake, the United States was still bound in honor to remain an ally of France.[22] But Hamilton believed that the United States was bound to act honorably toward France only so long as France acted honorably toward the United States. French ministers consistently violated American sovereignty. They attempted to manipulate American public opinion in order to pressure the new government to enter the war, or failing that, to allow France's navy and privateers to use American ports. Since France was seeking to exploit the new American republic for its own convenience, Hamilton saw no reason to adopt a generous view of American obligations to that country. Far from it: he was sure that such a view would lead Americans to become the pawns and dupes of France.[23]

To be sure, the United States owed its very existence to French aid; but the debt of gratitude applied to the old regime, not the new revolutionary government in France. Moreover, France had helped the United States not for benevolent reasons but to hurt England. American independence was payment in full for French services rendered during the American Revolution. Furthermore, it was unreasonable to expect gratitude to be very significant in relations between sovereign states. Even if the United States did owe some debt of gratitude to France, Hamilton believed that the "rule of morality" is different for individuals and states. Individuals may sacrifice their fundamental interests to pay off debts of gratitude because, generally, no one else is harmed as a result. In contrast, "existing millions and generations unborn" depend upon the decisions of statesmen. "Self-preservation," Hamilton observed, "is the first duty of a nation." If so, statesmen cannot sacrifice fundamental national interests to gratitude without violating their duty to their own people.[24]

Fidelity to Founding Principles

One might still argue that apparently common principles constituted some kind of obligation of honor from the United States toward France. How could Americans claim to be faithful to the principles of their own revolution, which are supposed to be universal, if they were willing to allow those principles to be undermined by the European monarchies that attacked revolutionary France? Since the demand that we be true to our founding principles underlies much discussion of American human rights and intervention policy today, Hamilton's response merits serious attention.

In the first place, Americans needed to look carefully before leaping to the conclusion that America and France, or America and any other revolutionary nation, shared the same principles. Whereas respect for natural rights generally led the United States to remain peaceful in its relations with other countries, the desire to proselytize for such rights led the French to attack many of the established governments of Europe. Hamilton denied that this ideological crusade was consistent with free government as Americans understood it. He also suggested that it was a mere device to enable France to establish a universal empire. If the United States joined France in this crusade, it would therefore betray rather than honor the principles of its own revolution.

Yet even if France and the United States had shared the same fundamental principles, Hamilton denied that this would have constituted an American obligation to aid France. According to the principles of the Declaration of Independence, peoples institute governments to secure their own rights, not the rights of everyone else in the world. Statesmen are trustees of the rights of their own people, not the rights of all men. Hamilton therefore concluded that "to vindicate its own rights, to defend its own honor"—these were causes for which a nation should hazard its very existence; but under no circumstances would it be honorable for American statesmen to hazard the existence of their country merely to defend the rights of a foreign people.[25]

The long-term implications of Hamilton's argument were best expressed in Washington's Farewell Address, which was largely written by Hamilton. Honor required good faith in the performance of existing alliances. Yet because today's allies are often tomorrow's enemies, it was essential to avoid permanent attachment to any country arising either from American sentiments or from treaty obligations. The fundamental lesson of the neutrality debate was that pursuing national interests without compromising national honor required limiting America's commitments to other countries while simultaneously developing its power as much as possible.

Significantly, neither Hamilton nor Washington believed that this grand strategy required an isolationist foreign policy. They recognized that the shifting sands of power might require Americans to form "temporary alliances" to provide for their security. Precisely because they resented previous American promises to France, they did not wish to shackle future American statesmen with a rigid doctrine from the past. Following Hamilton's lead, Washington actually advanced a nationalistic foreign policy. In principle, it allowed for a variety of economic, political, and even military agreements with other countries. Until or unless such commitments were necessary, however, it was prudent to focus on consolidating the union, economic growth, and territorial expansion in the West.

Both Hamilton and Washington knew that as time passed, the distance between Europe and America might begin to narrow, and the sources of conflict with European nations might begin to increase. Yet by then, they hoped, the United States, with a firm union, under an efficient national government, and with a people possessing virtually limitless wealth, would have the power to "choose peace or war, as our interest guided by our justice shall counsel." By then, they hoped, the United States would have the capacity to back up big words with big deeds.[26]

THE WAR OF 1812 AND NATIONAL HONOR

Backing up a nation's words with deeds depends upon its will as much as its capabilities. Though appealing to national honor is often necessary to develop the will to vindicate it, there are also serious dangers in appealing to a false or exaggerated sense of national honor. Those dangers are very apparent in the quarrels among the Founders over the appropriate policies for securing American maritime rights during the naval wars between England and France in the 1790s and early 1800s.

Both England and France attacked American shipping, and England impressed American sailors to man its navy. Americans believed these acts violated their rights and honor as an independent nation, but they had very different ideas about how to defend against them. Thomas Jefferson and James Madison feared that developing substantial military power would constitute an internal threat to American liberty, and perhaps even lead the United States into war. Therefore, after 1800, President Jefferson and his secretary of state, James Madison, developed a policy of peaceful coercion through economic sanctions. They hoped that boycotts and embargoes would enable them to vindicate American maritime rights while they systematically reduced American land and naval forces.[27] Insofar as they were willing to use sanctions, Jefferson and Madison demonstrated the will to defend American national honor; indeed, they put American honor at stake by employing sanctions against England especially. But the United States depended on England more than England on the United States. Their policy failed because their will to assert American rights and honor significantly exceeded the capacity of sanctions to influence the policies of England and France. After the sanctions failed, Americans believed they had no honorable way to retreat, and the United States went to war with England.

Yet because Jefferson and Madison were unwilling to develop military power, American forces generally fared miserably during the War of 1812, and President Madison failed to achieve his war aims. He failed to force the British to relinquish their alleged right to impress American seamen. Nor did the British agree to accept the principle that free or neutral ships made free goods, which Americans had a right to trade with all belligerents. New England almost seceded from the union as a result of this war. By waging war against England, the United States indirectly aided Napoleon, the greatest threat to peace and the independence of nations at the time.

Rights Worth Fighting For

Though Hamilton did not live to see this war, he could readily have predicted its causes and its outcome. It may be helpful to hear what he said about the dangers of allowing a false or exaggerated sense of national honor to guide American foreign policy. "True honor," Hamilton declared, "is a rational thing . . . as distinguishable from Quixoticism as true courage from the spirit of a bravo." True honor did not require going to war to vindicate just *any* American rights but only those that were certain and, under the circumstances of American weakness, essential to the young nation's existence. Hamilton did not believe the principle that free ships made free goods was one of those rights, for few nations accepted it at the time, and no great seapower would yield the right to prevent neutral shipping from reaching the ports of its adversaries. Impressment was indeed a serious violation of American rights, and one that merited arming to redress; but Hamilton knew that many seamen on American ships were British deserters. The British had a right to capture deserters and an absolute necessity to employ them in their fleets. The solution to the impressment issue, so far as there was one, was to develop provisions to return deserters to England, and to keep them off American ships.

If Americans had yielded the highly disputed right to trade with all belligerents and had found some means to accommodate England over impressment, they might well have avoided war with the nation most capable of doing their country enormous harm.[28] Had they understood honor as a "rational thing," they probably would not have gone to war with England in 1812.

Hamilton also observed that "true honor" could "never be separated from justice." It was therefore very distinct from jingoism, chauvinism, self-righteousness, and a "blind partiality to national errors." Though Americans had reason to complain about violations of their maritime rights, they had to admit that they too violated British rights by failing to comply with the Treaty of Paris. "Honor," Hamilton insisted, "cannot be wounded by consulting moderation." For this reason, "Nations ought to calculate as well as individuals, to compare evils, and prefer the lesser to the greater; to act otherwise, is to act unreasonably; those who counsel it are either impostors or madmen."[29]

Hamilton's major objection to the economic sanctions against England called for by Jefferson and Madison in the 1790s was that they might well provoke a war of national honor at a time when the United States was unable to wage such a war effectively. Hamilton was deeply sensitive to the honor of other nations that sometimes makes them willing to fight, even at the expense of their tangible interests. He believed that sanctions were little different from ultimatums. They are a last step before war because their purpose is to compel other nations to "submit to the disgrace or disrepute of having receded through intimidation." Against a proud and great nation like England, sanctions were bound to fail to achieve their objective. They wounded John Bull's pride more than they hurt his pocketbook, and John Bull was in a desperate struggle for survival against France.

Arm While Negotiating

It was far more prudent, Hamilton argued, to arm while negotiating, that is, to talk softly while preparing to defend the United States and its merchant fleet. This "two-track" policy had the merit of generating the military capability that was the only argument England was likely to respect at the time. It also demonstrated American national will without offending the British sense of honor. American negotiators might well acquire greater influence in England as their country's might increased. Americans would therefore have less need to retreat, and the British would still have some room left for compromise because an arms buildup was not an ultimatum that required them to defend their honor. Even if American influence failed to increase, Americans would not have to reprove themselves with having done nothing to defend their rights. They could hold their heads high, and then decide whether war was the appropriate option for settling the quarrel with England.[30]

Though Hamilton did his best to prevent the conflict with England from developing into a war over national honor, there were limits even to his patience. When war with England seemed likely during the Washington administration, he insisted that Americans were not "to crouch to any power on earth or tamely to suffer our rights to be violated. A nation capable of this meanness will quickly have no rights to defend."[31] In general, however, Hamilton's position was almost the mirror-image of the position of Jeffersonian adversaries. Because they sympathized with France and were generally hostile to England, they were very touchy about English affronts to American honor but more restrained about those arising from France. In contrast, Hamilton highlighted French insults and minimized those of England.

These converse positions were perhaps inevitable results of growing party conflict in the 1790s, but Hamilton believed there was both a moral and a strategic rationale for taking national honor much more seriously in American relations with France. In the first years of the Adams administration, France conquered most of Europe, the British navy was rife with mutiny, and England appeared to be bankrupt and unable to continue the war. If Napoleon's armies gained control of the British fleet, it looked as if the United States might have to stand alone against a European hegemon. At this time, France was attacking American ships at will and had seized hundreds of them. Lacking a navy, the United States was unable to defend itself. In the famous XYZ affair, Talleyrand, the French foreign minister, demanded a huge bribe merely to begin negotiations with Americans.

To avoid complete humiliation, Americans had to fight back; but fighting back required developing an army and a navy, and the will to use them. Though Hamilton hoped negotiations would produce peace, the necessity of preparing public opinion for an arms buildup and perhaps even full-scale war led him to portray the conflict as a test of American honor. "To capitulate with oppression," Hamilton observed, "is in any nation that has a power of resistance as foolish as it is contemptible. The honor of a nation is its life. Deliberately to abandon it is to commit an act of political suicide. . . . The Nation which can prefer disgrace to danger is prepared for a master." Worse, it may even "deserve one."[32]

NATIONAL HONOR IN THE TWENTIETH CENTURY

Why did Hamilton insist that "the honor of a nation is its life," so much so that he was even willing to commit the United States to wage war alone, without allies, against the nation that had overcome many of the greatest powers of his age? Was this statement merely rhetorical, or did it reflect something of continuing relevance to our time?

One possible answer, with important implications for discussions of American national honor in the twentieth century, was developed by Winston Churchill in his famous account of the "Tragedy at Munich" in 1938. Just before this crisis, France was allied to Czechoslovakia, and Czechoslovakia had mobilized some very formidable forces behind its defensive works. Had France stuck by its alliance with Czechoslovakia, Churchill was sure England would have sided with France if Hitler really intended to wage war to acquire the Sudetanland. Then the Germans would have faced a two-front war, and the German military, which did not believe Germany was ready for war, might well have overthrown Hitler. Yet Chamberlain and Daladier were so intimidated by Hitler's threats that they browbeat the Czechoslovaks into accepting the partition of their country. In Churchill's view, collapse of will in England and France led to a collapse of will in Czechoslovakia, which surrendered without a fight.

Though it is difficult to set out firm rules for the fog of war, Churchill suggested that there was one "helpful guide" for this sort of crisis: "this is called honor," which induces a "nation to keep its word and act in accordance with its treaty obligations." Churchill was well aware that the "pride which plays so large a part" in the inspiration of honor is in substantial tension not only with Christian humility but also with the egalitarian instincts and generally pacific tendencies of modern liberal democratic peoples. He also acknowledged that an "exaggerated code of honor leading to the performance of utterly vain and unreasonable deeds could not be defended, however fine it might look." Yet refusing to "look" base and weak, or perhaps better, desiring to appear strong and noble, seems to go hand in hand with the love of independence and liberty, so much so that it is perhaps impossible to encourage a spirit of resistance in a free people without appealing to their sense of their own honor and dignity.

Perhaps precisely for that reason, Churchill seemed to think that modern statesmen must bend over backwards to encourage a sense of honor in liberal democracies, which might otherwise react far too late to serious threats to their security. The path of honor in 1938 was both the path of duty and the only realistic hope for preventing war with Germany, or at least of waging war before the Germans became almost too strong to resist. By sacrificing the honor of their nations at Munich, Chamberlain and Daladier therefore came very close to committing what Hamilton called an act of political suicide. Poor Czechoslovakia, abandoned by its friends and convinced that resistance was futile, actually did commit suicide.[33]

Those who waged the Cold War always had Churchill's lessons of Munich in the back of their minds. All it took to make them think in Churchillian terms about honor and foreign policy was the perception that the Soviet Union was the second coming of the Third Reich. Then, no American statesmen believed they could yield to intimidation. None could afford to be accused of appeasement. This predicament sometimes led American Cold Warriors to practice the risky policies of brinkmanship. They also came to believe the United States had no choice but to seek its own safety through collective security agreements, first through the United Nations, and later through the complicated structure of alliances built during the Cold War. Credibility, or the will and ability to resist aggression and remain faithful to our allies, then became a virtual synonym for American national honor.

To borrow another phrase from Churchill, a case could be made that the Cold War was America's finest hour—finer even than Gettysburg and Normandy, because it was a much greater test of national resolve. While one may disagree about tactics at a thousand different places and times, the fact remains that the Soviet Union was at least as evil as Nazi Germany and was perhaps even more dangerous. It had to be contained, but as Tocqueville observed long ago, one should not count much on the capacity of modern democracies to endure great hardships or stick to their goals for a prolonged period.[34] Not surprisingly, in the twentieth century, the great question about American democracy was not its capacity to defend itself but its will to do so. Yet the United States stuck to one Churchillian, honor-based strategy for almost fifty years. "Stay the course," Ronald Reagan announced in another appeal to national honor as the Cold War approached its climax, and miraculously, that is what Americans did. Americans and their allies won the long struggle because they generally refused to be intimidated and kept their word. A sense of honor helped save the West.

Honor and the Vietnam Conflict

Unfortunately, there were theaters of the Cold War, such as Vietnam, in which an exaggerated sense of honor sometimes got the United States into trouble. Even granting that hindsight is twenty-twenty, there are good reasons to think that neither Hamilton nor Churchill would have pledged his nation's word to go anywhere, bear any burden, or pay any price in defense of freedom. Though catchy, the spirited rhetoric of Kennedy's inaugural address is a tragicomic caricature of the more sober views of Hamilton and Churchill. When those two statesmen invoked national honor as a justification for war, appeals to this intangible interest were always coupled with appeals to the vital security interests of their countries. They never went so far out on a limb that national honor by itself could justify a resort to war. Though many sought to show that American vital interests were at stake in the war in Vietnam, it is extremely difficult today to understand why anyone believed this. South Vietnam lost the war, and Indochina experienced terrible misery, but like the rabbit in the battery commercial, the rest of the free world keeps on going, and going, and going.

Those who study the lessons of history often seem condemned to misapply them. Vietnam in 1960 was not Czechoslovakia in 1938. The latter was vital to the West, both strategically and morally; the former was not. The most likely source of America's intervention in Vietnam was not a plausible strategic interest but a vague and bombastic Kennedyesque notion that Americans were bound in honor to secure freedom everywhere, even in countries where it had never existed before. Alas, once American troops were committed in large numbers in Vietnam, a sense of honor made it very difficult to leave when the conflict no longer seemed to justify the sacrifices in blood and treasure. The most likely reason it took so long for Americans to leave Vietnam is that they could not admit defeat. Since the beginning of the Cold War, every conflict with Communist governments had been portrayed as a test of national will. If Americans did not have the will to fight this war to the end, both their self-respect and their credibility with other, more valuable allies seemed likely to suffer. Sadly, the most compelling reasons for a slow and gradual withdrawal concerned the impact of withdrawal on our other allies, not on Vietnam itself. Quite pitifully, peace with honor came to mean peace without American humiliation.

"Vietnamization" supplied the decent interval that might plausibly have allowed defeat to be the responsibility of the Vietnamese rather than the United States. It allowed Americans to retain their pride at home and their credibility abroad. Perhaps this was the only way to withdraw from Vietnam with some semblance of honor, but the national humiliation and the self-deception of the Nixon and Ford administrations would never have occurred had Kennedy and Johnson been more clear about the requirements of national honor in the first place. Honor did not require defending freedom everywhere—certainly not where no serious strategic interests were at stake, and least of all where the people seemed to lack the will to fight for their own freedom.

Rational Honor Today

National honor therefore seems to have been the source, not only of the greatest success of American foreign policy in this century, but also of one of its worst failures. This makes it imperative to think carefully about Hamilton's view that "true honor is a rational thing." What could a "rational" sense of national honor mean today?

Rather than put words in Hamilton's mouth, perhaps we should reformulate the premises that underlied his efforts to conduct an honorable foreign policy. There had to be a balance between American words and American deeds. This balance required increasing American power, or moderating American claims, or both. Hamilton might therefore ask us some tough questions about what we think we are doing when we use or promise to use American forces today. What are we trying to achieve? Is the goal worth risking American lives and honor? Do we have the will and the means to achieve it? If not, can we develop them in time to make a difference? If not, are we making promises we cannot or do not intend to keep?

These questions might lead to caution in current discussions of expanding NATO in Eastern Europe. It is one thing to talk about including Hungary, Poland, and the Czech Republic in the Atlantic Alliance, and quite another to take the steps required to defend them without threatening the Russians or hurting further their already wounded pride. Yet unless we are willing to take these steps, NATO expansion may mean nothing at all, and could even undermine the Atlantic Alliance itself. If the Russians were ever to attack Poland, or the Czech Republic, or Hungary, would the West Europeans and the United States have the will to defend them? Or would they act the same way they did during the Hungarian and Czechoslovakian revolutions in 1956 and 1968? If the old members of NATO did nothing to help their new allies, would NATO remain credible among its older members?

If Hungary, Poland, and the Czech Republic are included in NATO, honor toward them requires making deterrence a reality in Eastern Europe. And honor toward the American people requires candor: a frank statement that new pledges might require stationing troops in these countries, or at least developing the capacity to get troops there rapidly. This may well be such a hard sell in Peoria that our president will not make the case for it; yet if he does not but also helps these countries become members of NATO, he may have set himself, our country, and our allies up for a humiliating fall. It makes considerable sense to say that the consequences of the Cold War are irreversible, that countries freed from the former Soviet empire cannot be taken back by a new Russian empire. Yet if we are not yet willing to back up new pledges with new deeds, perhaps we should not put our honor on the line, at least not until the time is ripe for developing the will and the capability to make these countries more than symbolic members of NATO.

Humanitarian interventions simply were not an issue in the Founding era, and we cannot be sure what any of the Founders would say about them today. Yet we know that Hamilton's candor made it difficult for him to make promises he did not intend to keep.[35] He might therefore question what we mean to accomplish in places like Zaire, Rwanda, Somalia, Haiti, and Bosnia. Is our goal to feed the hungry? Separate warring factions? Produce a stable peace? Build a nation? Institute a democracy? Selling interventions to Americans seems to require ambitious goals, but the more inflated our goals, the less likely we are to obtain them. In our country, popular support for humanitarian interventions is broad, but thin. In the age of televised violence, sometimes just a few dead or mutilated American soldiers are enough to send us packing.

If we are unlikely to have the will to stay the course in humanitarian interventions, perhaps it is more honorable not to intervene at all. We should not deceive ourselves or others: in many contemporary conflicts, we can do little more than put a Band-Aid on age-old wounds. Insofar as some interventions may do some good at no great risk to ourselves, there is some justification for them; but prudence would seem to dictate limiting our aims, declaring victory when we have accomplished them, and then getting out while our honor is still intact.

Any time more than the total strength of an American army division (around 20,000 troops) is committed to military operations other than war, one must also wonder about our priorities. Are they to prevent human suffering? Or are they to defend and advance the world order that the United States established in 1945 and fought for throughout the latter half of this century, an order that remains highly favorable to our interests and our principles? Like Charles de Gaulle, Hamilton had a sense of his nation's possible historic destiny. Eventually, the United States could develop the capacity to lead the free world in great struggles with aggressive powers far more dangerous than revolutionary France in his time, but to do so effectively it had to pick its fights carefully.

Although great-power conflicts disappeared with the end of the Cold War, there is no reason to think they are gone forever. There may be times in the next century when preserving our world order will require committing our will and our resources as much as we have in this century. It would be disgraceful for us to dissipate that will and those resources in conflicts unrelated to that fundamental objective. If we mean to address great conflicts in the next century as well as we have in this one, we would do well to think about Hamilton's grand strategy of limiting our commitments while increasing our capacity to honor them.

A Response

Robert Kagan

P rofessor Walling was absolutely right to identify in Hamilton a
very pronounced concept of honor, a concept that had a lot to do
with America's becoming a great power on the world stage. But having said that, I'd like to raise a few cautions about trying to derive
principles for American foreign-policy conduct in our own time from
the kinds of debates in which Hamilton engaged, for two reasons.
The first is that those debates have to be placed back in their political
context. A lot of what realists have seen as Hamilton's great insights
into foreign policy were really comments about how the world works
that were directed at a domestic debate. They were not meant to be
applied to foreign policy. The second and more serious caution is this:
Hamilton and the other Founders inhabited a very weak, fragile, and
relatively tiny country, newly born, in a world of vast powers, all of
which were capable of destroying it. Surely we must be careful about
applying strategies for conducting that tiny power's foreign policy to
the foreign policy of a great power—indeed, a superpower and the
world's sole superpower.

First, the problem of the political context. In the examples that Professor Walling drew upon and elsewhere in Hamilton, I find a certain

Robert Kagan is Alexander Hamilton Fellow at the American University
in Washington, D.C., a contributing editor of the *Weekly Standard*, and the
author of *A Twilight Struggle: American Power and Nicaragua, 1977-1990.*

97

inconsistency. It can be attributed, I think, less to fuzzy thinking about foreign policy than to the circumstances of the political debate in which he was engaged. An example is the passage Walling quotes from Hamilton's *Federalist* debate in which his main purpose was gaining the ratification of the Constitution. Hamilton set out a long list of dishonorable events that required ratification of the Constitution, mentioning specifically things that Britain was up to at the time, such as the occupation of posts in the Northwest territories in violation of the Treaty of Paris.

Two years later, after the Constitution had been ratified, Hamilton was secretary of the treasury and had as his primary goal putting America on a sound economic footing. He had very intelligently decided that it would be impossible to do this without good relations with Great Britain, and so you find him quite oblivious to the damages to American honor he had catalogued in 1787—so much so that in October 1789, before poor Thomas Jefferson had even managed to occupy his position as secretary of state, Hamilton was already negotiating behind his back with British emissaries and telling them not to worry. Friendship with Britain meant the most to him, and this was very sensible from his point of view.

So in 1789 we see a very pro-British Hamilton fighting a very anti-British Thomas Jefferson and James Madison, and many realists make the mistake of creating a Hamilton-Jefferson dichotomy with Hamilton the wise man and Jefferson the fool. In reality the two were engaged in a tactical dispute over how best to serve American interests. Jefferson thought that Britain's oppressive power had to be restrained and that the best way to do this was to have good relations with France, Britain's dire enemy, while Hamilton was saying, forget about France—our whole future is with Britain.

In the 1790s we see the rise of vicious partisan politics, and Jefferson has about 90 per cent of the American people on his side in defending France, in essence, while Hamilton is fighting a rearguard action. To me, it's ironic that Hamilton decided that honor was not the key issue in dealing with Britain's depredations on American shipping. But when it was France and the quasi-war— now *that* was worth sacrificing everything for, even though it was just as dangerous to take on France as it was to take on Britain. My point, again, is that in trying to find lessons from Hamilton it's important to keep in mind what he was really talking about. Most of his discussion was about how to shape American domestic society and not about foreign policy.

My second point has to do with looking at the foreign-policy musings of leaders of a very weak and vulnerable country and trying to derive from them lessons for our own time. On the matter of honor, it seems obvious to me that small powers understandably concern themselves less with questions of honor than with questions of survival. No one expects them to be engaged in a vast redeeming of honor at the risk of their survival. And of course, the *incapacity* to do anything about things you think are wrong means there's no dishonor in not doing anything. Again, it's standard realist practice to talk about John Quincy Adams and how we shouldn't go off in search of monsters to destroy and how nineteenth-century America was quite intelligently staying aloof from these matters. Well, perhaps staying aloof was an intelligent thing to do, but it also did not cast dishonor on the United States not to send its troops—its non-troops—across the Atlantic to do something about the oppression of Poland in 1830. American sympathies were very much with the poor Poles and with the Greek revolutionaries and with any number of other oppressed peoples in the nineteenth century. But honor was not at stake, because the capacity to do anything about these problems simply didn't exist.

What happens when power increases and the nation's role in the world increases is really the question we have to deal with today. At the turn of the century, when America emerged as a great power on the world scene, all of a sudden honor was much at issue. Teddy Roosevelt was engaged in a search for honor above all else. It was important to make sure the Dominican Republic could pay its debts, but at the end of the day that was less important to Roosevelt than for the United States to arrive at the position it was meant to have, in that sense fulfilling Hamilton's goals.

When America did begin as a great power to consider questions of honor, the principles that Americans have always stood for became part of what they meant by honor. Teddy Roosevelt, whom the realists raise up as the paragon of self-interested calculation, was the one who invented the idea of bringing civilization to the uncivilized Latins in our hemisphere. As a great power we should be in charge of what happens in our hemisphere. But as a great American power, we must remember that part of that charge is what Wilson said: teaching the people to elect good men. In a way that is the project that the

United States embarked on at the beginning of the century and has with important gaps fundamentally pursued ever since.

Certainly it is true that, as Professor Walling said, a nation's sense of honor and what it commits itself to should not outstrip its capability to carry out that commitment. And it is also important to remember that the definition of honor that Americans pursued in terms of spreading their principles, or at least supporting those who believed in those principles, was suppressed most seriously during times of greater strategic fears—certainly during World War II and to some extent during the Cold War. Today in the post–Cold War era, with all the major threats gone, the constraints on pursuing honor—defined as the support of principles that Americans believe are important—are less than they've ever been before. Whatever one may think about Bosnia, Haiti, and Somalia, the casualties we've suffered in these three operations combined don't equal what we suffer every year in military training exercises. And certainly the financial cost has not been great.

The predicament Americans find themselves in, then, is that their definition of honor, which since the turn of the century has led them to want to support certain sets of principles overseas, is now less constrained than ever, while the need to draw the line and say, *this* principle is counterbalanced by our fears of strategic adversaries, has eroded. It's no coincidence that not just under Bill Clinton but also under George Bush, the amount of international social work—or rather, the amount of honor-defending—Americans have done in increasingly remote parts of the world has been on the increase.

Notes

CHAPTER 1

"Honor, Interest, and the Nation-State"

Donald Kagan

1. Thucydides, *The History of the Peloponnesian War*, 1.76.2. The Greek words are *timê, deos,* and *ophelia.*

2. A. J. P. Taylor, *The Struggle for Mastery in Europe, 1848-1918* (Oxford, 1957), 491. For a critique of the Austrians' rationale for the policy see note 2 on the same page.

3. S. R. Williamson, Jr., *Austria-Hungary and the Origins of the First World War* (New York, 1991), 152.

4. D. C. Lieven, *Russia and the Origins of the First World War* (London, 1983), 141-42.

5. Sir Edward Grey, *Twenty-Five Years* (New York, 1925), 1:216.

6. Sir Edward Grey, *Speeches on Foreign Affairs 1904-1914* (London, 1931), 313.

7. Grey, *Twenty-Five Years*, 15-16.

8. Thucydides, *History*, 1.25.3-4.

9. George W. Baer, *The Coming of the Italian-Ethiopian War* (Cambridge, Mass., 1967), 4.

10. Ibid., 168-69.

11. Thucydides, *History*, 2.43.2.

12. Paul M. Kennedy, *The Rise and Fall of the Great Powers* (New York, 1987), 44-55.

13. Geoffrey Parker, "The Making of Strategy in Habsburg Spain: Philip II's 'Bid for Mastery,' 1556-1598," in W. Murray, M. Knox, and A. Bernstein, *The Making of Strategy* (Cambridge, Mass., 1994), 150.

14. Ibid., 149.

15. Ibid., 126-27.

16. R. M. Hatton, "Louis XIV and His Fellow Monarchs," in J. C. Rule, ed., *Louis XIV and the Craft of Kingship* (Columbus, Ohio, 1969), 160.

17. Jeremy Black, "Mid-Eighteenth Century Conflict with Particular Reference to the Wars of the Polish and Austrian Successions," in Jeremy Black, ed., *The Origins of War in Early Modern Europe* (Edinburgh, 1987), 232.

18. The quotations are from J. A. Lynn, "A Quest for Glory: The Formation of Strategy Under Louis XIV, 1661-1715," in Murray, Knox, Bernstein, *The Making of Strategy*, 184-87.

19. Ibid., 204.

20. Ibid., 185.

21. Fritz Fischer, "The Foreign Policy of Imperial Germany and the Outbreak of the First World War," in Gregor Schöllgen, ed., *Escape Into War? The Foreign Policy of Imperial Germany* (Oxford, 1990), 26.

22. Jonathan Steinberg, "The Copenhagen Complex," *Journal of Contemporary History* 1, no. 3 (1966): 42.

23. Lamar Cecil, *Wilhelm II Prince and Emperor, 1859-1900* (Chapel Hill, N.C., 1989), 300.

24. Hajo Holborn, *A History of Modern Germany, 1840-1945* (New York, 1969), 510.

25. Telford Taylor, *Munich, The Price of Peace* (New York, 1979), 229.

26. Correlli Barnett, *The Collapse of British Power* (New York, 1972), 366.

27. Taylor, *Munich*, 233.

28. Barnett, *Collapse*, 375.

29. Ibid, 549.

"A Response"

PETER W. RODMAN

1. Henry A. Kissinger, *A World Restored: Metternich, Castlereagh, and the Problem of Peace, 1812-1822* (Houghton Mifflin, 1957).

CHAPTER 2

"Honor as Interest in Russian Decisions for War"

WILLIAM C. WOHLFORTH

1. Donald Kagan, *On the Origins of War and the Preservation of Peace* (New York, 1995).

2. D. C. B. Lieven, *Russia and the Origins of the First World War* (New York, 1983). On contemporary expectations of relative power: W. C. Wohlforth, "The Perception of Power: Russia in the Pre-1914 Balance," *World Politics* 39:3 (April 1987).

3. Jack Snyder, *Myths of Empire: Domestic Politics and International Ambition* (Ithaca, N.Y., 1991).

4. For a sampling, see Robert Jervis and Jack Snyder, eds., *Dominoes and Bandwagons: Strategic Beliefs and Great Power Competition in the Eurasian Rimland* (Oxford, 1991).

5. See, especially, Jonathan Mercer, *Reputation and International Politics* (Ithaca, N.Y., 1996), and Ted Hopf, *Peripheral Visions: Deterrence and American Policy in the Third World, 1965-1990* (Ann Arbor, Mich., 1994).

6. Important recent examples include Snyder, *Myths of Empire*, and Charles A. Kupchan, *The Vulnerability of Empire* (Ithaca, N.Y., 1994).

7. Thomas Schelling, *Arms and Influence* (New Haven, 1966), 124-25.

8. Max Weber, *Economy and Society*, ed. Guenther Roth and Klaus Wittich (New York, 1968 [1922]), 2:904, 911. Cited in Randall Collins, *Weberian Sociological Theory* (Cambridge, 1986), 154, 158.

9. According to Martin Wight, *Power Politics*, ed. Hedley Bull and Carsten Holbraad (Leicester, England, 1978), chap. 8, "vital interest" replaced "honor" only in the late nineteenth century.

10. Carr quoted in Wight, *Power Politics*, 98. See in general the discussion in and sources cited by Robert Gilpin, *War and Change in World Politics* (Cambridge, 1981), 30-33. Practitioners of diplomacy frequently agree with this basic proposition. See Sir Harold Nicholson, *The Meaning of Prestige* (Cambridge, 1937).

11. See Martin Wight, *Systems of States*, ed. Hedley Bull (Leicester, England, 1977); and Adam Watson, *The Evolution of International Society: A Comparative Historical Analysis* (London and New York, 1992).

12. Richard Rosecrance, *The Rise of the Trading State* (New York, 1986), makes the case for this proposition.

13. For a brilliant analysis of the rules of the eighteenth-century great-power game in which Russia matured as a power, see Paul W. Schroeder, *The Transformation of European Politics* (New York, 1995).

14. Wight, *Power Politics*, chap. 3.

15. Skobelev claimed to be "avenging" the blow to Russia's honor and prestige caused by General Lomakin's defeat at the hands of the Tekke Turkmens in 1879. Quoted in C. T. Marvin, *The Russian Advance Towards India: Conversations with Skobeleff, Ignatieff, and other Distinguished Russian Generals and Statesmen* (London, 1882), 98-99.

16. William C. Fuller, Jr., provides a brilliant analysis of this constraint in *Strategy and Power in Russia, 1600-1914* (New York, 1992).

17. Collins, *Weberian Sociological Theory*, explicates Weber's theory of empire, prestige, and legitimacy, which is little known even among sociologists.

18. As James Fearon notes in connection with deterrence theory, "in choosing initially whether to threaten or to resist a threat, rational leaders will take into account observable indices of relative power and interests in a way that tends to neutralize their impact if a crisis endures. . . . The argument implies that observable aspects of capabilities and interests should strongly influence who gets what in international politics but that their impact should be seen more in uncontested positions and faits accomplis than in crises." "Domestic Political Audiences and the Escalation of International Disputes," *American Political Science Review* 88, no. 3 (September 1994): 758.

19. Two papers by Randall Schweller seek to reverse this bias: "Bandwagoning for Profit: Bringing the Revisionist State Back In," *International Security* 19:1 (Summer 1994); and "Realism and the Present Great-Power System: Growth and Positional Conflict Over Scarce Resources," in Ethan B. Kapstein and Michael Mastanduno, eds., *Realism and International Relations After the Cold War*, forthcoming.

20. For discussion and debate on these issues, see "The Rational Deterrence Debate," a special issue of *World Politics*, 41:2 (January 1989).

21. Fuller, *Strategy and Power*, chap. 9.

22. Richard Pipes, *The Formation of the Soviet Union* (Cambridge, Mass., 1964), 1.

23. Michael T. Florinsky, *Russia: A History and an Interpretation* (New York, 1955), 1:335, quoted in Robert C. Tucker, "Autocrats and Oligarchs," in Ivo J. Lederer, ed., *Russian Foreign Policy: Essays in Historical Perspective* (New Haven, 1962), 175.

24. Vasili Klyuchevsky, *Peter the Great* (New York, 1961), 270. Historians argue over whether Peter wanted Russia to become Western or merely wanted to use the West in order to beat it at its own game. (Cf. Florinsky, *Russia* 1:335.) But no one questions whether diplomatic equality with the European great powers was an objective. The aim

was that Russia, whether Europeanized or not, should take her rightful place among the most powerful states.

25. See, in general, M. S. Anderson, *The Rise of Modern Diplomacy, 1450-1919* (London and New York, 1993), who concludes: "When Peter died his country had been irrevocably launched into the mainstream of international relations in Europe" (71). Martin Wight also credits Peter himself with winning club membership in the victorious Great Northern War against Sweden *(Power Politics,* 46). Adam Wilson, "Russia and the European States System," in Hedley Bull and Adam Watson, eds., *The Expansion of International Society* (London, 1985), fixes the date as 1760, when "the despatches of Western ambassadors show that whatever they thought of the Russian world beyond, the Russian government had established itself as a European great power" (71).

26. Quoted in Fuller, *Strategy and Power,* 258.

27. Quoted in Barbara Jellavich, *Russia's Balkan Entanglements, 1806-1914* (Cambridge, 1991), 110.

28. A. J. P. Taylor, *The Struggle for Mastery in Europe 1848-1918* (Oxford, 1954), 82, 85.

29. Quoted in Jellavich, *Russia's Balkan Entanglements,* 172.

30. Fuller, *Strategy and Power,* 313.

31. Taylor, *The Struggle for Mastery,* xiv.

32. See Wohlforth, "Perception of Power," and Risto Ropponen, *Die Kraft Russlands* (Helsinki, 1968).

33. On Stalin's post-war vision, see Vladislav Zubok and Constantine Pleshakov, *Inside the Kremlin's Cold War: From Stalin to Khrushchev* (Cambridge, Mass., 1996), chap. 1.

34. Cyril E. Black, *The Dynamics of Modernization: A Study in Comparative History* (New York, 1966); Ernest Gellner, *Nations and Nationalism* (Oxford, 1983); Carlo M. Cipolla, ed., *The Economic Decline of Empires* (London, 1978); Gilpin, *War and Change in World Politics;* Alexander Motyl, "From Imperial Decay to Imperial Collapse: The Fall of the Soviet Empire in Comparative Perspective," in Richard L. Rudolph and David F. Good, eds., *Nationalism and Empire: The Hapsburg Empire and the Soviet Union* (New York, 1992).

35. V. I. Lenin, *Imperialism: The Highest Stage of Capitalism* (New York, 1968); Theda Skocpol, *States and Social Revolutions* (Cambridge, 1979).

36. On the Russian side, the war was probably a result more of expansionistic aims, poor decision-making, and a miscalculation of Japanese power than of concern for intangible interests. See Ian Nish, *The Origins of the Russo-Japanese War* (New York, 1985).

37. For a concise application to Russian and Soviet history, see Motyl, "From Imperial Decay to Imperial Collapse."

CHAPTER 3

"The Politics of Grandeur"

DANIEL J. MAHONEY

1. For the *locus classicus* of the realist constriction of the aims and ends of foreign policy see Hans J. Morgenthau, *In Defense of the National Interest* (Lanham, Md.: University Press of America, 1982).

2. See Kenneth Waltz, *Theory of International Politics* (Reading, Mass.: Addison-Wesley, 1979).

3. See Alexis de Tocqueville, *Democracy in America:* vol. 1, part 1, chap. 4; vol. 1, part 2, chap. 5, conclusion; and vol. 2, part 1, chap. 2.

4. For a fuller treatment of the thought and action of de Gaulle see my *De Gaulle: Statesmanship, Grandeur and Modern Democracy* (Westport, Conn.: Praeger, 1996). Several paragraphs of that book have been adapted and revised for use in this essay.

5. See Charles de Gaulle, *Memoirs of Hope: Renewal and Endeavor* (New York: Simon and Schuster, 1971), 200, 212, 227, and *The Complete War Memoirs of Charles de Gaulle* (New York: Simon and Schuster, 1967), 719-26.

6. For a representative statement of the Cold War as an episode in the age-old struggle for the European "balance of power" see de Gaulle's initial and qualified defense of the North Atlantic Treaty recorded by Claude Mauriac, *The Other de Gaulle, 1944-1954* (New York: John Day, 1973), 313-14.

7. On this point see Raymond Aron, *Memoirs* (New York: Holmes and Meier, 1990), 299.

8. Charles de Gaulle, *La France et son armée* in *Le Fil de l'épée et autres écrits* (Paris: Plan, 1990), 359-73. A flawed English translation appeared as *France and Her Army* (London: Hutchinson, 1945).

9. De Gaulle, *France and Her Army*, 28.

10. Ibid., 23.

11. Ibid., 28.

12. De Gaulle, *Complete War Memoirs*, 81.

13. De Gaulle, *Memoirs of Hope,* 189-90.

14. On Péguy and de Gaulle see my *De Gaulle*, 22-23, 34-35, 55, 65-66, 90, 140, 146-47.

15. Cited in Alexis de Tocqueville, *Selected Letters on Politics and Society*, ed. R. Boesche (Berkeley: University of California Press, 1985), 150-51.

16. The speech can be found in de Gaulle, *The Call to Honor: Documents 1940-1942* (New York: Simon and Schuster, 1955), 313-20.

17. De Gaulle, *Memoirs of Hope*, 178-79.

18. De Gaulle, *Complete War Memoirs*, 3.

19. Charles de Gaulle, *The Army of the Future* (Philadelphia: Lippincott, 1941), 15-21.

20. Stanley Hoffmann, *Decline or Renewal? France Since the 1930s* (New York: Viking, 1973), 191.

21. François Furet, Jacques Juillard, and Pierre Rosanvallon, *La République du centre* (Paris: Colmann-Lévy, 1988).

22. Pierre Manent, "La démocratie sans la nation?" in *Commentaire*, no. 75 (Autumn 1996), 571-72.

23. De Gaulle, *Memoirs of Hope*, 183.

24. Ibid., 194-95.

25. On Mitterrand's acceptance of the flawed but nonetheless "socialist" character of the East European Communist regimes and his hatred of all forms of resurgent nationalism see Bernard Lecomte, "François Mitterrand et l'Europe de l'est: le grand malentendu" in *Commentaire*, no. 75 (Autumn 1996), 577-83.

26. See Habermas's essay, "Citizenship and National Identity: Some Reflections on the Future of Europe," in Ronald Beiner, ed., *Theorizing Citizenship* (Albany, N.Y.: SUNY Press, 1995), 255-81.

27. Martha C. Nussbaum, *For Love of Country: Debating the Limits of Patriotism*, ed. Joshua Cohen (Boston: Beacon, 1996).

28. Manent, *"La Démocratie,"* 573.

29. See my discussion of Aron's analysis of "the dawn of universal history" in my *The Liberal Political Science of Raymond Aron* (Lanham, Md.: Rowman & Littlefield, 1992), 17-72.

30. Pierre Manent, "On Modern Individualism," *Journal of Democracy*, January 1996, 8.

31. Raymond Aron, *Clausewitz: Philosopher of War* (Englewood Cliffs, N.J.: Prentice-Hall, 1985), 410.

32. De Gaulle, *The Edge of the Sword* (New York: Criterion, 1960), 7-10.

33. André Malraux, *Felled Oaks: Conversations With de Gaulle* (New York: Holt, Rinehart and Winston, 1972), 123-24.

CHAPTER 4

"Alexander Hamilton on Honor"

KARL WALLING

1. Hamilton to the *New York Evening Post*, 8 February 1803, in *The Papers of Alexander Hamilton*, ed. Harold G. Syrett (New York: Columbia University Press, 1961-79), 26:82-85.

2. See Frederick W. Marks III, *Independence on Trial: Foreign Affairs and the Making of the Constitution* (Wilmington, Del.: Scholarly Resources, 1973), and his "American Pride, European Prejudice, and the Constitution," *The Historian* 34, no. 4 (August 1972).

3. See Locke's "Second Treatise" in *Two Treatises of Government*, ed. Peter Laslett (Cambridge: Cambridge University Press, 1988), 145-48, 365-66.

4. Marks, *Independence on Trial*, 3.

5. "Federalist" 15 in *The Federalist*, ed. Jacob E. Cooke (Middletown, Conn.: Wesleyan University Press, 1961), 91-92.

6. Nathan Tarcov, "War and Peace in *The Federalist Papers*," unpublished paper for the Liberty Fund Colloquium on *The Federalist*, Claremont, Calif., 12-15 January 1989.

7. "Federalist" 3-4, pp. 13-23, and "Federalist" 80, pp. 534-41.

8. "Federalist" 3, p. 18.

9. See, again, Tarcov, "War and Peace in *The Federalist Papers*."

10. "Federalist" 4, pp. 20-21; 11, pp. 65-71; 23, p. 147; and 70-77, pp. 471-521.

11. "The Essays of Brutus," in Herbert J. Storing's *The Anti-Federalist: Writings by Opponents of the Constitution*, ed. Murray Dry (Chicago: University of Chicago Press, 1985), 112, 143-47.

12. See Ralph Lerner, "Commerce and Character: The Anglo-American as a New Model Man," in his *The Thinking Revolutionary: Principle and Practice in the New Republic* (Ithaca: Cornell University Press, 1987), 195-221.

13. See "Federalist" 1, p. 2; 14, pp. 88-89; and 39, p. 250.

14. See Max Farrand, ed., *The Records of the Federal Convention of 1787* (New Haven: Yale University Press, 1966), 1:402.

15. "Federalist" 62-63, pp. 420, 422-23.

16. "Federalist" 11, p. 72.

17. Ibid., 73.

18. See Jefferson's "Opinion on the French Treaties" in *The Portable Jefferson*, ed. Merrill D. Peterson (New York: Penguin Books, 1977), 268-80; and James Madison to Thomas Jefferson (with attached Draft of Country Resolutions), 2 September 1793, in Marvin Meyers, ed., *The Mind of the Founder: Sources of the Political Thought of James Madison* (Hanover, Mass.: Brandeis University Press, 1981), 195-99.

19. See Forrest McDonald, *Alexander Hamilton: A Biography* (New York: Norton, 1982), 265-70.

20. Alexander Hamilton and Henry Knox to George Washington, 2 May 1793, in Hamilton's *Papers* 14:372-84. See also McDonald, *Alexander Hamilton*, 271-72.

21. Hamilton to Washington, 2 May 1793; "Pacificus" 3, 6 July 1793; and "Americanus" 1, 31 January 1794, in *Papers* 14:401-7; 15:67-72, 671-72.

22. Jefferson, "Opinion on the French Treaties," 274.

23. "Reasons for the Opinion of the Secretary of the Treasury and the Secretary of War Respecting the Brigantine Little Sarah," 8 July 1793, in Hamilton's *Papers* 15:74-79.

24. "Pacificus" 2, 3 July 1793; "Pacificus" 4, 10 July 1793; and "Pacificus" 5, 13-17 July 1793, in Hamilton's *Papers* 15:59, 92-95. The distinction between public and private morality may help explain why Hamilton was willing to risk his life in a duel of honor. As an individual, he had a right to risk his life because the consequences of his action were limited to himself and his family. As a statesman, he had no right to risk the survival of his nation for the sake of national honor, unless its independence and most fundamental rights were also at stake. Though the duel cost Hamilton his life and his family a father, Hamilton believed he had no choice but to accept the challenge of Aaron Burr. In Hamilton's time, it was dishonorable to refuse a challenge and equally dishonorable to kill a man in a duel. He believed his political career would have ended both if he declined to fight and if he killed Burr. Personal motives (Christian restraints on dueling, and the death of his first son in a duel in which Hamilton forbade him to shoot at his challenger) also made it virtually impossible for Hamilton to shoot at Burr. As a result, he stood his ground, resolved to fire in the air, and paid the price. (See Hamilton's *Papers* 16:278-80, 282, 334-40.)

25. "Pacificus" 6, 27 July 1793, in Hamilton's *Papers* 15:131-33.

26. See Washington's "Farewell Address" in *The Annals of America* (Chicago: Encyclopaedia Britannica, 1968) 3:614.

27. For the best discussions of party conflict, ideology, and foreign affairs during the administrations of Jefferson and Madison, see David C. Hendrickson and Robert W. Tucker, *Empire of Liberty: The Statecraft of Thomas Jefferson* (New York and Oxford: Oxford University Press, 1990), and Lance Banning, *The Jeffersonian Persuasion: Evolution of a Party Ideology* (Ithaca and London: Cornell University Press, 1978).

28. "Philo Camillus" 2, 7 August 1795; "The Defense" 3-7, 29 July–12 August 1795; "The Answer," 8 December 1796; and "Conversation with Robert Liston," October 1797, in Hamilton's *Papers* 18:518; 19:90-92, 99, 105-7, 116-19; 20:434; and 21:307-8.

29. "The Defense" 5, 5 August 1795, in Hamilton's *Papers* 19:90-92.

30. Hamilton to Washington, 14 April 1794, and "The Defense" 5, 5 August 1795, in Hamilton's *Papers* 16:271-72; 19:90-92.

31. "The Defense" 2, 25 July 1795, in Hamilton's *Papers* 18:498-99.

32. "The Warning" 3, 21 February 1799, in Hamilton's *Papers* 20:520.

33. See Winston Churchill, *The Gathering Storm* (Boston: Houghton Mifflin, 1948), 319-21.

34. Alexis de Tocqueville, *Democracy in America*, trans. George Lawrence (New York: Harper, 1969), 1:221-30.

35. Honor also requires good faith toward the American people. President Clinton was forced to choose between two promises—to the Bosnians and to his own people. He postponed his decision until after the election of 1996, but rather than leave Bosnia without producing something that at least looked like a stable peace, he broke a pledge to Americans to withdraw by the end of 1996. This cannot but fuel cynicism about his honor and make it more difficult to obtain support for sustaining the Bosnian intervention or beginning other interventions in the future.

Index of Names